REINVENTING TEXTILES

Volume Two
Gender and Identity

Edited by Janis Jefferies

TELOS

Edited by Janis Jefferies
Commissioning Editor: Matthew Koumis
Proof reader: Vivien Brett & Katherine James
Reprographics by Studio Technology, Leeds
Typeset and printed in Malta by Interprint

Published by
Telos Art Publishing
PO Box 125
Winchester
SO23 7UJ
telephone: +44 (0) 1962 864546
facsimile: +44 (0) 1962 864727
e-mail: editorial@telos.net
www.arttextiles.com

© Telos Art Publishing 2001

ISBN 1 – 90201510 – X

A CIP catalogue record for this book is available from The British Library.

Notes: all dimensions are shown in metric and imperial, height × width (× depth).

Photo Credits
James Anderson, John Dean, Isaac Applebaum, Stephen Pitkin, James Isberner, Tim Thayer,
Peter Clark, Cheryl Bellows, Michal Kluvanek, Audrey Mandelbaum, Grete Balle, Borch
Jacobsen, Jenny Hansen, Colorgruppen, Ivan Binet.

Supported by

Editor's Acknowledgements

I would like to thank all the contributors for their thoughtful and challenging essays, as well as all the artists, photographers and lenders whose work is illustrated in this book. Special thanks are also due to Sarat Maharaj who gave permission for his essay 'Textile Art – Who are You?' to be reproduced in this anthology. I originally commissioned it for an international art textile project that I was involved in as part of a steering group that included Kay Lawrence, Sharon Marcus, Ruth Sheuer and Aleksandra Manczak. The project culminated in an artists' professional retreat in Poland, 21–27 June 1992. The project was called *Distant Lives/ Shared Voices* and Maharaj's contribution was published in the document as part of a collection of artists' pages and four other commissioned essays.

I would like to thank John Gange and Michael Nagelbach for their assistance. I am particularly indebted to Alison Raftery for her invaluable copy editing skills and insightful annotations on all of the essays. She helped me survive the late night sittings and consume delightful Indian meals in the process. Thanks are also due to all those involved with Telos Art Publishing for bringing this project to completion. Matthew Koumis has been more than patient in recognising the complexities of preparing a multi-authored and international publication. This new anthology consolidates *Reinventing Textiles: Tradition and Innovation* (1999). I am grateful to Professor Sue Rowley for the opportunity to promote the growing interdisciplinary inquiry into textile in the expanded field of visual and material culture. As exemplified by the first volume, *Reinventing Textiles: Gender and Identity* brings together artists, writers, historians, theorists and curators from many places and regions of the world.

Janis Jefferies

Publisher's Acknowledgements

The initial idea for this series emerged during a chance meeting between myself and Diana Drummond over a rather dubious curry during a conference organised by the European Textile Network in Manchester in 1996. I have since tried to track Diana down to thank her, but the trail went cold at a New York restaurant where she worked – if you are reading this Diana, I would love to say hello! Anyway, this concept was then fleshed out during a lengthy and entertaining e-mail correspondence with Professor Sue Rowley in Sydney, whose book *Craft & Contemporary Theory* (Sydney: Allen & Unwin, 1997) I was and remain very impressed by. Sue came up with our title *Reinventing Textiles*, and the excellent first volume. The baton has since passed to Janis Jefferies, who has surpassed my high expectations, and then on to the very safe hands of Dr Jennifer Harris for Volume 3 which is already in preparation. I am well aware how enormously time-consuming it is to edit each book, but there is clearly an urgent need for intelligent probing of the many layers of inspiration beneath international contemporary textile art.

I would like to take this opportunity to thank David Kay and Keiren Phelan at Southern Arts for their enthusiasm, trust and financial support, and the many people who have helped this book along its way at the production end, including Vivien Brett, Jacqui Taylor, David Hyde at Celsius, Sue Leahy, Paul Markham and Joe Bonnici. Many thanks to all the writers, artists and photographers for their labours of love, and to you the reader – we're making a good team.

Matthew Koumis

Essayists' Acknowledgements

Mariette Bouillet and Giorgia Volpe would like to thank their translator Tanya Morand as well as Jean-François Boisvert, Yvan Binet, and Renée Méthod.

Alison Ferris would like to offer many, many thanks to Peter Coviello, Amy Honchell, and particularly Anne Wilson for their insightful comments regarding her essay.

Sunjung Kim would like to thank her translator Lee Youngjun, and Kim Sooja for her collaboration in the project.

Barbara Layne would like to thank Karen Michelsen and Janet Bezzant.

Kay Lawrence would like to thank Dr. Diana Wood Conroy who read and commented upon her text.

Victoria Lynn would like to thank Nalini Malani for her collaboration in the project.

Tina Sherwell would like to thank Wildad Kawar for permission to view and photograph costumes from her collection.

The kind co-operation of several public galleries, museums and owners of work illustrated is acknowledged, including the Museum of Contemporary Art, Chicago, REVOLUTION, Detroit and New York, and the Art Gallery of South Australia.

CONTRIBUTORS

DR. RENEE BAERT is a critic and curator, whose essays on contemporary art have been widely published. Recent exhibitions include *Trames de Mémoire* (Expression and Canadian tour, 1996-8). Other writings centred on clothing-based artworks include *Materializing Memory: The Clothing Works of Faye HeavyShield (n.paradoxa,* winter 1999), *Three Dresses, Tailored to the Times (Material Matters,* YYZ, 1999), and 'Skirting the Issue' *(Screen,* vol.1.35, no.4, 1994). She lives in Montreal, where she teaches in the MFA programme at Concordia University.

MARIETTE BOUILLET was born in 1973 in France. After completing a masters degree in literature, she moved to Quebec City where she still lives today. As a multidisciplinary artist she explores video art, documentary, theatre, performance art, music and scenography. Poetic writing holds a major place in her work. She also writes critical texts.

ALISON FERRIS has been the curator at the Bowdoin College Museum of Art in Brunswick, Maine since 1996. Previously, she was a curator at the John Michael Kohler Arts Center in Sheboygan, Wisconsin, where she organised a series of exhibitions that combined an exploration of materials with that of social and cultural issues. Most recently she organised *Skin and Bones: An Installation by Polly Apfelbaum* (2000), an exhibition and catalogue featuring new work by Apfelbaum.

PETER HOBBS lives in Montreal. His art has examined gay identity, national identity, tourism and narrative. He exhibits internationally and across Canada. His work is interdisciplinary and includes installation, performance, video and textiles.

JANIS JEFFERIES is Reader in Textiles in the Department of Visual Arts, Goldsmiths College, London. In 1996 she was awarded a Betty Park critical writing award in textiles. She has exhibited internationally, curated exhibitions and written for many magazines and books worldwide, including 'Yinka Shonibare: Dressing Down Textiles in a Victorian Philanthropist's Parlour' in *Reinventing Textiles: Tradition and Innovation* (Telos Art Publishing, 1999), and 'Textiles: What can she know?' in *Feminism and Visual Culture* (Edinburgh University Press, 2001).

SUNGJUNG KIM was born in Seoul in 1965. She is Chief Curator at the Artsonje Museum, Kyongju and Artsonje Center, Seoul, Korea. Since 1993 she has been a visiting lecturer at many universities in Seoul including Sang-Myung Women's University. She has curated several major exhibitions of contemporary visual art in Korea, Japan and Australia including *Slowness of Speed* at the National Gallery of Melbourne and the Gallery of New South Wales.

KAY LAWRENCE is a visual artist, writer and senior lecturer at the South Australian School of Art, University of South Australia. In 1981 she initiated the community tapestry movement in Australia. As well as exhibiting extensively in Australia and overseas she has completed a number of major public commissions, including a tapestry for Parliament House, Canberra in 1988, for which she was made a member of the Order of Australia.

BARBARA LAYNE is an artist and Associate Dean in the Faculty of Fine Arts at Concordia University in Montreal, Quebec. Her work incorporates the Internet as a place to collect, transmit and exchange textile information as a part of studio arts practice. Recent projects that use textiles and digitised images include *Electronic Textiles: Hacking the Museum* (1996), *webs://textiles and new technology* (1998) and *Textiles/TECHSTYLES* (1999).

GREG KWOK KEUNG LEONG was born in Hong Kong where he worked as a teacher, in radio and as an arts administrator before emigrating to Australia in 1981. He retrained as a visual artist, but has continued to undertake consultancies in the arts. In 1997, he directed an Australian Government Evaluations and Investigations Program research project, culminating in the publication, *Towards Internationalising Art School Curricula*. He has exhibited widely in Australia. His work examines both the personal and the wider political issues related to being a gay Chinese Australian.

VICTORIA LYNN is Curatorial Manager of the Australian Centre for the Moving Image – Cinemedia, Melbourne. She has written and curated the contemporary arts of India since 1993 when she organised the exhibition *India Songs: Multiple Streams in Contemporary Indian Art* for the Art Gallery of New South Wales, Sydney. She was curator of Contemporary Art at the Art Gallery of New South Wales from 1987 to 2000. She has also worked extensively with contemporary Australian and international contemporary arts and regularly publishes in journals and magazines.

SARAT MAHARAJ is Professor in Art History at Goldsmiths College. Born and educated in South Africa, he was given refugee status in Britain. His work engages issues relating to cultural translation, textile practice, multiculturalism and difference, as evidenced in *The Duchamp Effect* (MIT Press, 1996), *Global Visions* (Kala Press, 1993) and the Sydney Biennial (1997). His most recent work explores 'Dislocutions: Interim entries for a dictionnaire elementaire on Cultural Studies' in (ed) Jean Fisher, *re-VERBERATIONS: Tactics of Resistance: Forms of Agency in Transcultural Practices* (Jan Van Eyck Akademie Editions, 2000).

LINDSAY OBERMEYER is a visual artist who employs the history and metaphors surrounding textile practices to study issues of gender, identity and representation. She has exhibited her art throughout the USA and internationally, and has been active in using the arts to change the manner in which illness is perceived and treated. She is currently working on a book that examines mental illness and its effect on family and society.

DR. TINA SHERWELL was born in England. She is the Director of the Archive of Palestine Art, Al-Wasiti, and currently lives in Jerusalem. She has completed a Ph.D on Palestine Art and popular culture and has published articles on the subject and books, including 'Bodies in Representation: Contemporary Arab Women's Art' in *Contemporary Arab Women's Art: Dialogues of the Present* (Women's Art Library, 1999). She has curated several exhibitions of contemporary Palestine Art in Israel and abroad.

LISBETH TOLSTRUP is a teacher and textile designer and has studied History of Art at The University of Aarhus since 1997. After being head of a teachers' design college 1985-8, she became the co-owner of a graphic design studio. She exhibits at numerous solo and group exhibitions, has edited and published articles, essays and catalogues about Danish and international design, avant-garde and textile art, and is the author of several books.

GIORGIA VOLPE was born in 1969 in Sao Paulo, Brazil, and in 1993 founded the Piratininga Cooperative Studio, Sao Paulo. She has developed her visual work in print and photographic media, installation, textiles, and body-action, investigating corporal, affective and sensory images. She has participated in shows and exhibitions internationally. In 1998 she moved to Quebec City and completed a masters degree in visual art at Laval University. She is now a member of the Administration Conseil of Centre Vu and resident artist of Atelier de Création, Méduse, Quebec.

ANNE WILSON is a practising artist whose work incorporates found cloth and hair to explore themes of time, loss, and private and social rituals. She has shown extensively, and her art is in the permanent collections of several museums in the USA. Wilson is currently a Professor in the Department of Fiber and Material Studies at The School of the Art Institute of Chicago.

CONTENTS

xiv

LIST OF ILLUSTRATIONS

Colour plates

Introduction: Textile Transitions

Janis Jefferies

'A text is made up of multiple writings, drawn from many cultures and entering into mutual relations of dialogue, parody, contestation, but there is one place where this multiplicity is focused and that place is the reader, not as hitherto said, the author.... A text's unity lies not in its origin but in its destinations.'[1]

Place, location and position offer roots for the metaphoric use of textile as a material set of practices and processes and as a mobile set of signs. For this collections of essays I invited artists, writers, historians, theorists and curators who find themselves living in (but not necessarily coming from) cities in England, Denmark, Israel, Korea, Pakistan, United States, Canada, Quebec and Australia to consider how textile metaphors and signs have informed their diverse practices. As a consequence, a variety of writing styles can be detected and they range from the highly personal to the highly academic. A number of approaches have also been pursued and these range from letters and interviews between artists and their stories of travel, migration, the crossing of borders and nomadism to an analysis of dress and identity, cloth and the body, sewing as machine. Each author has drawn on a number of other disciplines such as cultural and literary theory, post-colonial debate and psychoanalysis to unravel the complexities of gender, body and identity as they mark divergent routes in textile history and contemporary practice. Each contributor has drawn on textile as a primary medium of cultural knowledge and experience.

Why then 'Textile Transitions'? As a working dictionary definition, transition indicates a passage of travel from one state to another, while the idea of translation (literally as some essays have been 'translated' from one language to another) entails a form of encounter that is different and independent of the original. As Benjamin noted, the task of the translator is always a fraught one and (inevitably) there will always be a 'somewhat provisional way of coming to terms with the foreignness of languages' in the feel and structure of the essays that follow.[2] This is particularly noticeable in Lisbeth Tolstrup's discussion around the problems of interpreting and naming divergent textile practices that have historically informed debates within the Nordic scene.

The anthology opens with an essay written by Sarat Maharaj in 1992. 'Textile Art – Who are You?' stages a number of ideas around centre and margin, place and identity, body and representation, gender, sweated labour, displacement and diaspora. The question of who are you is 'translated' into the question 'Textile Art am I you? 'As reworked in his recent writing, Maharaj insists that we pay attention to all the 'unknowns' that are travelling with bundled belongings, as waves of enforced nomadism exacerbate conditions of statelessness across Europe.[3] An autobiographical anecdote powerfully narrates his grandmother's experience of recycling war surplus parachute silk fabric in the Apartheid land of the South Africa of his youth. We are shifted from any romantic idea of silk, which is at one and the same time both woven in some faraway colonial place and quilted by gendered labour in English sweat shops. We are implicated as witnesses to the stories of textile transitions in journeys that do not return us to some mythical dream of lost homelands or ambivalent site of production and fixed cultural identity.

Greg Kwok Keung Leong's essay examines the palpable tension between the cultural identities we construct for ourselves and those that are constructed for us. The tension is textually and visibly mapped through the two cultures that his mother was born into and the costumes that she wore – Chinese and Australian. By telling her story, he is able to 'translate' his experiences of diaspora into the details of personal narrative and national political debate to produce *Remembering Chinese*, a series of indeterminate garments that are conspicuously gendered. The elaborate embellishments of traditional dress can be re-read as sites for subversive argument about gender, body and national identity. Tina Sherwell takes up this point in her analysis of how ideas of the motherland are negotiated and represented through Palestinian costume, the popularity of embroidery and national perceptions about the role of women and their bodies.

In Victoria Lynn's discussion of the work of Nalini Malani, the association of textiles with nation and narration is inextricably linked to the colonial encounter. Lynn contends that Malani does not promote a fixed Indian identity through dress but uses the sari to question the effects of globalisation on local ecology and on the female body. Both Lynn and Leong cite Elizabeth Wilson's seminal work on dress and identity to propose that dress is the frontier between the self and the social and its mediations of the body. Her writing, together with that of Elizabeth Grosz and Kaja Silverman, informs Renée Baert's theoretical inquiry into the practices of Cathy Daley and Glynis Humphreys (amongst others) whose clothing works act as surrogates for the body. Few objects, Baert argues, have the mnemonic force and bodily aura of clothing: it is the very tissue between self and the social, the psychic and social boundaries. Alison Ferris draws our attention to the qualities of 'forbidden touch' that she perceives in the cloth and stitch works of Anne Wilson.

In her artist's statement, Wilson describes her current practice as an 'abstract topography suggesting mapping and navigation, both internal and external to the body'. Cloth invokes skin and memories of the tactile but it can also hide a wound. At the threshold of the body, a wound speaks of mortality, a theme that opens an exchange of letters between Kay Lawrence and Lindsay Obermeyer. Obermeyer's over-scaled, knitted garments explore the question of identity as inseparable from the relationship between herself and her daughter; a relationship determined by the very mortality of the mother's body and the cycle of loss that is central to experiences of subjectivity.

Lawrence links her child's understanding of gender difference to the loss of 'Mother' as a sign for plenitude and completeness. For both of these artists, the rhythms of their bodies are interwoven with their experiences of motherhood and are connected through the processes of their respective textile practices in knit and weave.

The role of 'Mother' as a sign for abundant generosity is pursued in Peter Hobbs' essay as he recalls his earliest memories of the machine on which his mother sewed clothes, sheets and curtains for the family. As he observes, sewing and gay aesthetics for him became embedded in the context of a queer needle, its powers and possibilities vis-à-vis questions of sexual difference and gender.

The needle as critical tool and healing implement is reconfigured in the latter works of Kim Sooja. Her need for material and spiritual survival is a personal one. As observed in Sunjung Kim's essay, it can be traced to her earliest memories of sewing blankets with her mother when all of her senses, thoughts and activities coincided with one another. In this experience, she discovered that so many memories, pains and affections of life lie buried and unnoticed. A feeling of identity between the cloth and the artist is evoked 'while the former is being sewn'; and a curious nostalgia evoked by those things. Kim Sooja bundles up the traditional wrapping cloth of Korea (bottari), piles it high on a truck and travels across the cities of Korea and Europe. She expands the notion of 'home' and the politics of location from the domestic to the public sphere. The contradictory feelings of 'home' and 'away' are expressed through a curious nostalgia and nomadic trajectory.

In 'Thread of Passage', Mariette Bouillet describes the metaphoric, tactile images of Giorgia Volpe as imbued with her experiences as a perpetual dweller in nomad territories. In her work, sensorial memory is revived through the clothing of others. Through their odour, stain and smell, clothes carry traces of another life, embedded with stories of the migrant limbs that were once housed within their folds. Bouillet remarks that the foreigner changes you and changes themselves in relation to mutation and exchange of clothes. Transformed objects find temporary resting places and suggest the possibility that you might live *somewhere*. Barbara Layne's migrant textiles, comprising her collection of Maya textiles and personal belongings, are bundled and carried from Mexico through America to Canada. The cultural baggages of which she writes are sometimes light and sometimes heavy with systems of classification. In the digital cargo with which she now concerns herself, Layne contends that digitisation is just one further stage in a continual process of translation in which textiles are physically displaced from their 'orginiary' museum classification and transmitted through the internet. Textile becomes a sign representing acts of migration and relocation in virtual places where no freeze-frame of 'motherland' exists.

I hope it will be apparent from this introduction to an extraordinarily rich range of essays that I do not wish to propose rediscovery of gender, body and identity as forms of fundamentalism nor forms of textile that are confined to predetermined nomenclature. Each contributor challenges familiar assumptions and adopts an open and fluid (but not unquestioning) approach to these issues.

I have proposed that ideas embedded within the theme of 'Textile Transitions' are in dynamic process. As musically connoted, transition is a movement between one key and another during which something changes from one state to another. The world as seen from one's own place is dismantled; and as seen from another is reassembled. Any reclaiming of territory that fixes our identities into an exclusive, closed and essentialised map is undone. How the past is seen, grasped as history, told and narrated, grasped as memory and bodily shifted recognises the primacy of textile in the construction of knowledge and cultural production. As readers we may encounter an eclectic freefall in our travels as text and textile move through multi-layered interpretations to no final destination.

Notes

1. Roland Barthes, *Image-Music-Text* (London: Fontana, 1977) p. 147.
2. Walter Benjamin, 'Task of the Translator' in *Illuminations* (London: Fontana Press, 1992) p. 75.
3. Sarat Maharaj, 'Dislocutions: Interim entries for a dictionnaire elementaire on Cultural Studies' in (ed) Jean Fisher, *re-VERBERATIONS: Tactics of Resistance: Forms of Agency in Transcultural Practices* (JanVan Eyck Akademie Editions), 2000, pp. 32–48.

TEXTILE ART – WHO ARE YOU?

Sarat Maharaj

1. The century's boxing match. A knockout roar of muscle across the stadium. Eubanks strides towards the ring. A spotlight chases after him, half catches up, jig-dances over him, speeds ahead. What's he got on?

A smock, a long T-shirt or kaftans cut off at the thigh? Hi-tech medical gown, an A-line mini, blouson or Grecian rustic tunic? Rough-hemmed towelling, chemise, loose-fit cheesecloth, cling-film muslin, frayfringe.... What seems like 'manly swagger signs' switch into 'womanly sway signs' and back again. A shuttle sets up between them, to and fro. Neither one thing nor the other, it seems to be both. We face an 'indeterminate garment'.

2. An 'undecidable' – as Derrida puts it, something that seems to belong to one genre but overshoots its border and seems no less at home in another.[1] Belongs to both, we might say, by not belonging to either. Should we comprehend 'Textile Art' under the chameleon figure of the 'undecidable'?

3. We stand in front of Duchamp's *Genre Allegory*.[2] Two regimes of seeing hold us in their grip, a deadlock of two genres and their discourses. A cloud of cloth bulges out of the canvas frame, ready to tear away, to cascade out of it. A laddered fabric moulded into lumpy form, half-sagging, half-tumescent. Perhaps it was once a crackling sheet of stiffening for collars and cuffs, dazzle tissue-lining which evaporates as it's ironed – a yard of moiré, a 'fusible'. As we look, cloth seems to run away from itself, playing on its own thread and threading, 'spinning out its own yarn'. We are called to look on it as if at a painting, but one without paint and pigment. Cloth stages the syntax of its own forms and textures. We are struck by its sheer 'painterliness'.

Against this 'pure formalism', the pieces read as 'history painting'. Duchamp stretches and shapes the cloth so that it suggests a profile portrait of George Washington, a star-spangled flag or blood-soaked gauze, a drenched bandage. It speaks of the scars and wounds of war – the violence out of which nation, patriotism, politics is carved out. Cloth serves as sign, stands in for something else. Duchamp ties it in quite an arbitrary, factitious way with idea of war and conflict, as 'emblem' of it. It becomes symbol, hurtles away representing something other than cloth, triggering off yet another stream of associations. We are in the allegorical mode – an excess of signs.[3]

In the Duchamp piece, therefore, cloth is all even as it is nothing. It is everything, 'bare stuff and fabric', that set off a visual dynamic for formalist ends. At the same time, it is nothing as it effaces itself to serve as figure or cipher for some idea or concept, for programmatic ends. The two genres play off against each other, citing and cancelling out each other in an unending tussle between them.

4. 'Supreme Quilting Co.' – before us a photo of a bleak, redbrick building slinking sideways out of view. It might be Southall or the Midlands, even North England in the 1970s. In front of the building, Asian women in winter coats over their traditional salwar/kameez. Women from the Punjab, what journey from the green, dusty countryside into the centre of the modern? Some are holding up placards, some huddle up to a fire in a drum, a makeshift brazier. A mythic scene of workers on strike in the machine age, marking out the site of dispute and disagreement – conditions of work, labour and production.

However much the 'quilt' aspires to the state of 'artwork', it does not shake itself free of references to the world of making and producing. Hung up on a wall, framed, put on display, it catches our attention as statement of form, colour, texture. We soar away with its allusive, narrative force. But we never quite manage to set aside its ties with the world of uses and functions, with the notion of wrapping up, keeping warm, sleep and comfort, some feeling of hearth and home. In all of this, it is no less easy to blank out memories of its links with the domain of processes, crafts, and techniques.

Half-on-wall, half-on-floor, it stand/lies/hangs before us: everyday object and artwork in one go. Domestic commodity which is at the same time the conceptual device. The quilt stands/lies/hangs before us as a speculative object without transcending the fact that it is a plain, mundane thing. Not entirely either and yet both, an 'undecidable'.

Meyer Vaismann, Haim Steinbach, Jeff Koons – the everyday consumerist object aspiring to the conditions of artwork while adamantly holding onto its brute mundaneness? Is it simply a calico mattress-divan or has the shift of context made of it an object for another kind of attention? Has the quilt not always straddled such a double-coded space, an ambivalent site of this sort?

5. It seems at odds with Greenberg's view, pre-eminent amongst the classic modernist stances, that genres should be clear cut, self-contained, their boundaries crisply defined and meticulously patrolled. Each genre pares itself down to the textures and logic of its own medium – holding check on the drive towards spilling over into another.

6. 'O busy weaver, stop. One word, why these endless labours? One moment speak. But no, the shuttle flies and the figures emerge floating from the loom, from the rolling mill, from the vats admitting not a second's interruption. You would say that production wishes more and more to mime perpetual motion, to draw near the heart of nature which establishes us here. We who contemplate the factory are deafened by its humming. It is only when we envelope death. Death weaves life. I am the image. I am the carpet.'[4]

7. The silk might have been woven in some faraway, colonial place. Few knew where. An ancient craft for the most modern of things. Bales of it were brought over, cut up, fashioned into parachutes somewhere in Britain. Where exactly? Hems and seams, who stitched the parachutes together? At once delicate fabric and tough engine of war. Sacred cloth and airforce material – floating, lifesaving and death-dealing umbrella.[5]
     War surplus, the shift to tough synthetic material, few knew how these silk parachutes came to be sold off in faraway Apartheid land. Lying opened out in the courtyard, like some creature wounded and brought down, last gasps of its billowing, wavy forms stretched flat across a vast carpet of sinewy hessian sacks basted together. My grandmother carefully cutting into the silk, close along its panelled seams and edges, folds and joins, reclaiming yard upon yard for some other uses.
     At once sacred cloth and object of warfare, life saving and death-dealing engine – now run up as shirts, pants, skirts and saris for us, the ragged of Apartheid land. For us, on that Apartheid shore – aliens, colonial subjects, soon to be called 'Burghers van die Republiek'. Soon to be cast out as 'the exiles', then to arrive as 'immigrants', then to live as non-nationals, forever

non-citizens – belonging by not belonging, neither insiders nor outsiders, 'swarthy resident aliens' always?[5]

Textile Art am I you?

Notes

1. Jacques Derrida, 'Living on Borderlines', in *Deconstruction and Criticism*, pp. 75–176.
2. *Genre Allegory* may be described as an assemblage work made of cloth, nails, iodine and gilt stars. It is held within a private collection in Paris.
3. Walter Benjamin, *The Origin of German Tragic Drama*, p. 174.
4. Jean Baudrillard, uncited source.
5. Lyotard & Monory, *Récits Tremblants*, p. 119.

THE DRESS: BODIES AND BOUNDARIES

Renée Baert

In her book *Imaginary Bodies,* the philosopher Moira Gatens has used this title to describe the often unconscious ways that social beings interpret bodies and the values and qualities inferred to them.[1] The imaginary body, she argues, is the key to deciphering how male and female biologies come to have meaning as historically and culturally specific masculinities and femininities.

Of particular concern in her analysis is the cultural imaginary of the female body. 'The female body, in our culture', she writes, 'is seen and no doubt often "lived" as an *envelope, vessel* or *receptacle.* The post-oedipal female body, to paraphrase Freud, is first a home for the penis and later for a baby'.[2] Gatens argues that the social construction of women as partial, incomplete, lacking boundaries, castrated, serves to undermine their status as ethical and political subjects. Women are not seen to have integrity 'precisely because they are not thought of as *whole* beings'.[3] As Gatens leads us to understand, the resonance of imaginary understandings of the partiality of the female body relative to the imagined wholeness and integrity of the masculine body extends metaphorically into the realm of ethics. It is further reproduced in the cultural imaginary of the body politic itself, where the masculine figure remains the privileged designator of the human.

Gatens specifies that the imaginary body is not simply a subjective phenomenon of imagination or fantasy; rather, it is a social product, culturally specific, and refers to 'those images, symbols, metaphors and representations which help construct various forms of subjectivity'.[4] Indeed, she specifies, there is not a singular social imaginary – an ideology – but rather a plurality of social imaginaries.

The concept of the imaginary body shifts our view away from a body understood in terms of biology or anatomy – a body given in nature.

Rather, it is a cultural body, invested with libido and significance. Gatens' argument acknowledges her debt to Luce Irigaray's foundational analysis of a structural isomorphism between *logos*, the phallus and masculine form, one that operates an exclusion of feminine specificity, which remains unrepresented and unthought. Jane Gallop, also following Irigaray's argument, advances this point when she states that 'phallomorphic logic is not based on anatomy but, on the contrary, reconstructs anatomy in its own image'.[5]

The concepts of the imaginary bodies and morphological configurations that these writers identify reveal how our ideas of bodies are construed through psychic investments, symbolic renderings and representational supports. But, as Elizabeth Grosz notes, the body 'is an open-ended, pliable set of significations, capable of being rewritten, reconstituted, in quite other terms than those which mark it, and consequently capable of reinscribing the forms of sexed identity and psychical subjectivity at work today'.[6]

In what follows, I want to draw upon contemporary art practices by women artists who have been working with clothing as a surrogate for the body. In particular, I want to refer to works which in various ways distort – by expanding, contracting or otherwise manipulating – the morphology of the female form. I'd like to explore how the use of distortions of the boundaries of the female body in such work might serve to intervene in the congealed residues of the cultural imago of women, to figure another relation to signification and desire.

As modes of figuration, morphological elaborations can serve to highlight the relation between the forms by which the body is depicted and the meanings these enable. If morphologies of the body are already abstracted from anatomical or biological mimesis, and if one can imaginatively apprehend the body through metonymic figural analogues, I want to suggest that the plasticities of art may provide a particularly cogent means through which to signify women's embodiment and its psychic registrations from an alternate vantage to the conventions described by Gatens.

As a wide range of art practices have long revealed, the depictions of corporeal distortions can readily convey the emotive powers of the body, that is, the disjuncture between the body as it might be measured anatomically or physiologically and the body of affect – the feeling body. My principal focus, however, is more specifically on how the clothing works that are my subject here may also have something to say about the psychic and social parameters of the female subject, whose body as a representational site is already over determined, always already caught in a vast network of signification from which it is crucial to negotiate some form of retrieval. Clothing, precisely because of its juncture between the body and the social, its linking of corporeality and culture, can be utilised as a medium through which to speak to the contradictory sites of femininity.

Kaja Silverman has observed that clothing, in articulating the body, articulates the psyche. So how might we interpret the destabilisation of conventional body boundaries in the clothing works by so many women artists working today? Although exceptions might be cited – notably, for instance, Charles LeDray's under-scaled figures – contemporary clothing-based works by male artists have generally tended to conform to the scale of the human body. This has been far less true in the work of women artists (whose work with the medium of dress also far exceeds that of their masculine counterparts). Rather, it is not unusual to encounter works of exaggerated height or scale, which may play upon the assimilation of stature to cultural value, status and even myth: such as Christine Lofaso's *Shift*, a paper dress hanging at a height of over 2 metres (7 feet) and printed with a text from Freud's *Dora: An Analysis of a Case of Hysteria*, or Anne Ramsden's 2-metre (7-foot) *Dress!*, a glamorous evening gown of emerald satin, of a narrowness defying any bodily fit; or Sylvat Aziz's monumental standing sculptures of chador-clad figures, rendered in copper, or Beverley Semmes' exorbitant 'larger than life' dress sculptures. Or works may be diminutive, such as Aganetha Dyck's 'shrunken' clothing, or impossibly thin, such as Cathy Daley's 'skinny' dress-sculptures, or virtually anorectic, such as works by Maureen Connor in which inner female garments are stretched tight over steel armatures. Or the boundaries of the body may not even be discrete, such as with Beverley Semmes' *Watercoats*, two dress forms joined as one corpus, or the inter-bounded body forms in works by Naomi London and others: artworks that raise questions that circulate around psychic boundaries, split subjectivities and the psychic residue of the complex negotiation for the feminine subject of her separation from the *corps-à-corps* with the maternal object. Or the body forms depicted through clothing may be transparent, or porous, or floppy, or rigid, and so on.

In such works, distortions are employed to expand, contract, render transparent, join or otherwise manipulate the female form. In a certain sense, this is not so unusual. Throughout its history, what has fashion in Western culture done but constantly change, indeed fabricate, through dramatic transformations and fluctuating ideals, how we 'see', and thus 'live', that body? But the morphological manipulations of these artworks,

Cathy Daley: **Little Black Dress** (2001)
fabric
5 x 1m (17 x 3ft)

with their concomitant destabilisation of body boundaries, also propose
figurations whose valences hold particular psychic registers vis-à-vis the
cultural 'imago' of the female body.

So I want to raise issues about the cultural imaginary of the female body with particular reference to ideals and understandings of the feminine form, about conceptions of the boundaries of the female body vis-à-vis psychic space and social space; and, in my reading of works by Jana Sterbak, Glynis Humphrey and Cathy Daley, about the power of 'surfaces' as a means of conveying subjectivity in its articulation with corporeality.

One of the best known, not to say notorious, dress works in contemporary art today is doubtless Jana Sterbak's *Vanitas: Flesh Dress for an Anorectic Albino* – the so-called meat dress. The work is composed of 23 kilograms (50 pounds) of raw flank steak, the jagged edges sewn together to shape the 'cut' of a simple, elegant dress. The meat is fitted to a standard dressmaker's form – that is, to the ideal shape of the female body – but is a body turned inside out.

The patchwork dress of marbled meat hangs torso-to-torso with the viewer, in a perverse rendering of fashionable wear and consumer display. The title *Vanitas* initially invites the work to be viewed from within the art historical tradition of these allegorical tableaux, in which signifiers of mortality – perishable fruit, burning candles, time pieces, skulls and the like – are set amidst the depicted opulence of material bounty and earthly beauty. The Vanitas have traditionally served as cautionary meditations on the ephemerality of life and the transience of material pursuits and carnal temptations, recalling the viewer to the spiritual necessity of overcoming the hungers of the flesh.

And what of the hungers of the anorectic? Typically female, the anorectic lives a state of starvation, even to the point of death, seeking a triumph over the needs of her body, and more specifically seeking to rid herself of the 'fleshiness' that marks her body *as* female. Elizabeth Grosz has described anorexia as 'a form of protest at the social meaning of the female body'.[7] Through a fierce determination, the anorectic strives to shrink the rounded female form culturally associated with feminine passivity and accommodation. It is the very layer of *flesh* that the anorectic disowns that Sterbak's gross dress proffers up, an undelectable epidermis. For what is Sterbak's *flesh dress* if not a sardonic rendering of the female body – female flesh – as meat – as commodity, as an object put on display to various orders of consumption. And with this, concomitant implications of how the sexually specific body/flesh of women is intertwined with female psychical identity – as indeed it is in the operations of displacement of the anorectic to which the title refers.

Underpinning the concept of the Vanitas is the Christian dualism between earth and heaven, body and soul, which are viewed as discrete and incompatible spheres. But the concept of the body image, as it has been elaborated in clinical psychoanalysis and neurological studies, already bespeaks – in contrast to this dichotomy – the interdependency of body and mind. Thus the anorectic's attempt to overcome the body through extreme measures of discipline, even as it partakes of inherited notions of bodily renunciation and transcendence, is itself an enactment of the inter-implication of body and psyche: a visual theatre, with its emaciated player, of unconscious conflicts – conflicts that arise around the cultural contradictions of women's sexual identity and play out through her shrivelling form.

As disturbing as the dress is when it is first displayed as fresh meat, it is as it shrivels and dries that it becomes a yet more radical and repulsive sight, pulling taut against – tearing from – the underlying form, its juices evaporating, its flesh reduced to a tough thinness, its colour darkening, its marblings of fat thickening and hardening into protruding veins. In its enlistment of the element of time, the work registers another dimension, producing a potent symbol of the aging, 'degenerating' woman as she is culturally identified: that is, as a kind of horror, the abjected antithesis of the feminine ideal of youth and beauty.

As a female form mediated through the protocols of art, *Vanitas* is at the furthest possible remove from the ideals of harmony, structure and composition that finds its apotheosis in the classical nude. This body is not a body contained and static, not an object – a 'still life' – for the dispassionate view that is ever, as Lynda Nead has suggested, in danger of sliding over into the field of desire.

This figure, as if with its insides out, imperils the very notion of boundaries and containment, and even desire. The object troubles borders of various kinds: it is body and dress, inside and outside, animal and human, its contours in a state of flux, its acrid odours permeating the space around it. As a 'dress', the object compounds clothing, fashion and body. As Karen Hanson has observed, however, and which the decaying *flesh dress* instantiates, there is another side to the corporeality that fashion at once covers over and identifies: the mortality that is its end. 'As our clothing is testimony to our embodiment', Hanson writes, 'it can whisper of the actual material death that, as humans, we may rather seek, in vain to avoid'.[8] And so we return to the Vanitas, in *our* time, however, not as an allegory for transcendence and the overcoming of the body, but as a figure for the body as a 'real', as a limit point of will and desire.

In Glynis Humphrey's *Gorge* (see colour plate 13), the disquieting excess implied in the exaggerated scale and volume of the work is already given in its title. To say the suspended garment is oversized is certainly to understate the case: the dress is 4.6 metres (15 feet) in height, 2.75 metres (9 feet) wide, with a hemline circumference of 13.4 metres (44 feet); it comprises about 400 metres (438 yards) of voile fabric and it weighs some 113 kilograms (250 pounds). The association of the title, reinforced by the scale of the work, is immediate: to gluttony, to inordinate appetite. Though but a few letters short of the more felicitous descriptive, gorge-ous, the gorging female is precisely its cultural antithesis, an abjected figure of excess, out of measure.

If the anorectic body signifies conflicts that turn upon the cultural norms of femininity, the obese body is no less a deviation from these norms, in which food and nurturance assume particular symbolic 'weight'. Susan Bordo argues that food is an invested site wherein a 'double bind' governs the construction of femininity. The 'rules' – subtended by advertising and other representation vehicles of the cultural imaginary – require women 'to construe any desires for self-nurturance and self-feeding as greedy and excessive' and demands of them that they contain and control their hungers. 'The control of female appetite for food', Bordo writes, 'is merely the most concrete expression of the general rule governing the construction of femininity: that female hunger – for public power, for independence, for sexual gratification – be contained, and the public space that women be allowed to take up be circumscribed, limited'.[9]

Produced to an exorbitant scale, *Gorge* does what is culturally discouraged, in some instances even disallowed, to women: it takes up space – lots of it, breaking with the constricted psychical and social boundaries most generally allocated to women. The absent figure drawn by the dress, however, is rendered, but for its scale, to a conventional proportion. It is not a figure suggestive of fleshly corpulence, nor is it a grotesquerie. Indeed, the strapless evening gown, enlarged from a women's dress pattern to a size 66, is modelled along the pleasing lines of a 50s-style party or prom dress. The giant, out of scale, out of bounds appetites to which the title refers, then, and as Bordo suggests, are not ones to be satiated by food. The figure stands 'larger than life', mythic, suggesting, through both scale and title, an embodiment of hungers, desires, appetites of a proportion that would greatly expand the compass of women's normative allocation. The inordinately sized dress work might be seen to at once evince a claim – to more, and more – and to embody a threat: the archetypal threat of the devouring woman.

The bodice frame, of grid wire, is covered with a peach-toned, waterous silk-like fabric, while the crinoline frame, of wire and hoops, holds ten tiered crinolines with double layered, translucent, peach/flesh coloured voile skirts. A sprung steel cable fashioned to act like a spinal cord, allowing the dress a certain animation, to turn and to undulate when touched, suspends the entire dress. The coloration of the work – a very close approximation of Caucasian skin – together with its animation effects, suggest another, considerably more mediated, 'flesh dress'. The colour tones of the garment inter-references fabric and flesh, suggesting clothing as a cover, which 'makes' the body, yet the body, always the animate of its wear.

The colossal size of the dress dwarfs the spectator, who is placed in a scale relation reminiscent of a child's physical proportion to the maternal body and, even more to the point, to its psychic apprehension of the omnipotence of this figure. In its inaugural installation, set in a stairwell at the Art Gallery of Mt. St. Vincent University, in Halifax, Canada, the garment filled the entire space, requiring of the viewer – and upsetting not a few of them in the process – that they push their way through and out of the voluminous 'skin' of these skirts and crinolines in order to enter the gallery. Elsewhere, the garment has been hung from the ceiling by pulleys, and the viewer, this time by choice, may enter under its billowing skirt.

Either way, to enter the skirts is to be surrounded, womb like, by the soft dome of fleshly peach encompassed in its sensual surfaces. More threateningly, the work, with its uterine/vaginal 'gorge', may call forth fantasies of dangerous maternal omnipotence, unconscious fears of engulfment, of a regressive merging with the maternal body, recalling the role of the phallus in differentiation, in revolt and separation, in overcoming, beating back, maternal power. Yet for both sexes, the maternal body is also the original site of *jouissance*, a *jouissance* that must be repressed in order to accede to civilisation and the Law of the Father.

The maternal figure, however, provider of the All to others, her body literally and symbolically fed upon, suggests another axis of meaning of the work, proposing another axis of who is gorging and what is being gorged upon. As Jessica Benjamin has described, the mother is a profoundly desexualised figure; she is 'provider, interlocutor, caregiver, contingent reinforcer, significant other, empathic understander, mirror.... She is external reality – but she is rarely regarded as another subject with a purpose apart from her existence for her child'.[10]

As Benjamin describes, Freud's much-quoted question, 'What does woman want?' implies another: '*Do* women want?' or 'Does woman have a desire?' If, as she argues, the hallmark of femininity is precisely the lack of sexual agency, in her revision of Freud's question, Benjamin shifts its focus from the woman as object of desire, *what* is wanted, to the matter of the subject of desire, she who desires (ibid. p. 86). Glynis Humphrey's clothing sculpture – a body form both maternally and sexually connotative, possessed of a sensual inner chamber, enlarged to uncommon scale, fabricated through a metaphor of flesh, provocatively titled – not only registers, in the most emphatic terms, the matter of female *presence*, but with this, complex nuances that circulate around precisely such questions of giving, wanting and being.

Cathy Daley's extensive and ongoing series of *Untitled* drawings (see colour plate 14),[11] which first began to appear in 1994, and have since expanded to include sculptural works, present a morphology of dress inspired by the iconographies of female glamour found in high-fashion magazines and in the studios of a vintage Hollywood. Daley's depictions of an extensive series of gowns and skirts proceed in an extravaganza of designs, an energetic proliferation of models of elegance and flair.

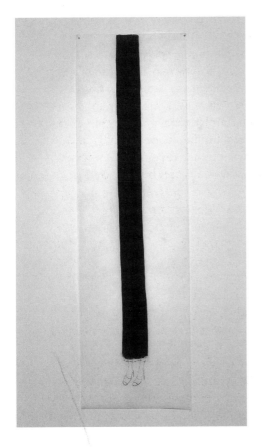

Cathy Daley: **Untitled** (2001)
pastel on vellum
320 x 91cm (126 x 36in)

These robes, most life-size, are drawn with sweeping, confident movements of black oil pastel on translucent white vellum. The series includes full-length gowns impossibly long and slender, with looping pin thin straps; voluminous skirts that supersede the bodice almost entirely; crinolined gowns and form-fitting sheaths with ruffles or Spanish flares or ostrich feathers; circle skirts opened in twirling motion, the exposed legs in animated movement; an array of shoulder-baring bodices over skirts of every kind. The dresses charge the empty white field with all the charisma of icons, while the vivid strokes of Daley's lines also lend them a sense of movement and verve. These are images made to the measure of desire, idealised and unattainable.

The shapely figures depicted by Daley are a quotation of the female body reconstrued to a more fanciful proportion. They are an overcoming of anatomical literalness to reimagine the contours of the body in terms of affect and gesture, to figure a host of movements and moods that are materially externalised through the expressive garments. As phantasmatic objects, however, these robes are also rooted in representation and its mediations of the body. They derive from inherited stereotypes of glamour, residual traces of former ideals, contemporary 'classics' of the feminine. If Daley's drawings proffer a semiotics of feminine glamour divorced from any day to day of women's existence, her use of familiar sources, whose representations of femininity are a forceful presence in the cultural imaginary, highlights how such representations shape the contours of identity. The datedness of the dress styles, with its trace of nostalgia, situates the images in the field of memory, yet memory imprinted by a social iconography that is itself annexed by fantasy. In drawing (literally) this mental impress of the past into the present, Daley raises entirely contemporary issues concerning the female body as spectacle and object of voyeurism, the merchandising of the female body and the inextricable links between image and identity.

Alison Ferris has observed that, 'clothing's role … is to display a unified "identity" while in reality holding together an always fragmented "self" '.[12] Marks, traces and unfixities in the visual field of the drawings work against such stabilising effects, thwarting an idealised identification and compromising the seduction effects of the garments. The very changeability and multiplicity of the forms of Daley's works, in both her drawings and sculptures, like the endless overturnings of fashion, figures the feminine as unfixed. The ambivalence that circulates around this fashion iconography – the pleasure and refusal so interimplicated in Daley's work – finds an echo within feminist thought, between its forceful critique of the fashion industry on the one hand, and, on the other, the recognition of fashion as an object of pleasure, an embodiment of fantasy and a vehicle of play.

There is an uncertain tension between the appeal of these gowns and a resistance to their allure. This effect is produced by several elements that conspire to undo the ego ideal of the perfect dress. Most immediately apparent is the very excess of the rendering of the garments, an exaggeration that highlights their illusory quality. (This is a feature of the drawings and of the sculptures – such as a stretch knit dress of a circumference of some 13 centimetres (5 inches), or floppy black patent leather shoes of gigantic proportion.) This departure from the stable ideal, the already available cultural image, is furthered through the lack of definition or coherence in the contours of the garments and their attenuated and otherwise altered shapes. But the most notable interference in the drawings occurs in their margins. The translucent white vellum, far from a neutral backdrop to set off the garments, is marked with smudges and carryover strokes of oil pastel, besmirching the surface field. The reminder of a 'real' body – the artist's body – incorporated through the residual marks and traces of her movements and exertions is a counterpoint to the fantasy body implied by the dress. It is as if the simple iconography of the dresses is but an alibi for the vivid, vigorous, sweeping gestures of the artist. In these works, the body absent from these empty dresses is itself displaced to the margins, to the field of the unrepresentable. Writing on the concept of the female imaginary, Margaret Whitford has suggested it might be found in the 'scraps' and undersides of representation, a point of possible relevance here.[13] These semiotic traces, without any real shape or form of their own, form a body signature, embedded in the tissue: a limit-point of transcendence, a defile of the unity and self-sameness of the image, a corporeal infiltration of the 'real' into the field of representation.

The 'flesh/skin' of meat, the 'silk/skin' of fabric, and the 'tissue/skin' of vellum: in the works of Sterbak, Humphrey and Daley, there is a direct allusion to the irreducible corporeal basis of existence, to the complex psychic interimplication of bodies and being. The plastic materialities specific to visual art serve in the work of these artists to constitute analogues for the materiality of the body. These material properties rejoin the metaphoric quality of clothing as a 'second skin', a membrane that separates and joins, that surrounds and divides. Like skin, clothing is a border: a boundary that at once joins and divides. It is inside and outside, body and culture – yet a boundary whose demarcations are by no means stable.

Further, by evoking the female form, mediated through its clothed attribute, the works, rather than refusing the 'object' status of women, operate on the other side of the equation; that is, they introduce, through the cultural properties and phantasmatic powers that adhere to clothing, as well as through the expressiveness of the garments, a mode of *subjectification* that operates on the side of women.

In working *through* the image of the female body, yet modifying its parameters, adjusting its boundaries, denaturalising the image, and generally subjectifying the 'absent' body that is yet referred to through the delegate of clothing, these works may have an effectivity in abating the power of the unconscious cultural imagoes of sexual difference, a power that holds its effectivity precisely because it is so naturalised.

The dress works by Sterbak, Humphrey and Daley exteriorise the female form through an expressive morphology, altering its conventional scale and boundaries, and producing a figuration that depends less on direct anatomical resemblances than on analogies and imaginative association. In this respect, they seem less to convey 'the body' in any generic sense than, more complexly, female embodiment in its lived, affective, multivalent, cultural and phantasmatic dimensions.

Notes

1. Moira Gattens, *Imaginary Bodies, Ethics, Power and Corporeality*, London and New York: Routledge, 1996.
2. Ibid. p. 41.
3. Ibid.
4. Ibid. p. viii.
5. Jane Gallop, 'The Body Politic', in *Thinking Through the Body, p. 94.
6. Elizabeth Grosz, 'Volatile Bodies', in *Toward a Corporeal Feminism, pp. 60–61.
7. Ibid. p. 40.
8. Karen Hanson, 'Dressing Down Dressing Up: The Philosophic Fear of Fashion', p. 234.
9. Susan Bordo, 'The Body and the Reproduction of Femininity', in *Gender, Body Knowledge*, p. 18.
10. Jessica Benjamin, *The Bonds of Love, Psychoanalysis, Feminism, and the Problem of Domination, p. 23.
11. An earlier version of this discussion of Cathy Daley's work appears in my curatorial essay for the exhibition catalogue, *Trames de mémoire*, Ste. Hyacinthe: Expression, 1996.
12. Alison Ferris, *Discursive Dress*, p. 3.
13. Margaret Whitford, 'Luce Irigaray: Philosophy in the Feminine', p. 119.

THE THREAD OF PASSAGE: GIORGIA VOLPE

Mariette Bouillet

'Once you wear a shirt or a pair of shoes for a long time, the destiny of these objects unites with yours. Man shapes what he wears to his own image; it becomes part of him. He abandons part of himself to it.'

Maria-José, Mother of Saints, Rio de Janeiro

It was a spring day just after her first winter passed in Quebec City that I met Giorgia Volpe. I immediately had the impression that I had known her forever, in a meeting that was to mark a friendship and a complicity of two strangers in a foreign country. Giorgia had just left Brazil for an artist's residency here at Vu[1] and I had lived here for only a few months. We were each fascinated by the work of the other and the links that united us. This period corresponded with a transitory, exploratory phase, at times in her life and at times in her practice, in which I now perceive more clearly the troubling dimension. The discovery of a new country, a new city, new landscapes and new faces was inextricably and mysteriously linked for her with her development of a medium with which she was already familiar: photography. During this first winter passed in Quebec, from the white outside to the darkroom, Giorgia wandered alone in the streets, in the cold and the snow taking black and white photographs with which she perfected her printing techniques. Looking at her photographs I was confronted with my own impressions of this snowed-in city, whose photographic essence was revealed to me in a striking way. I think of this somewhat anguished feeling that one can sense in a suspended, frozen, still time, of the impression of finding oneself in a city of ghosts, silhouettes, shadows, that disappear and reappear, and also of the sensation of an unreality of place, an effacement of the senses by the snow which in its whiteness renders the landscape monochrome, erases footsteps, confuses pathways, softens sounds, masks colours and smells. Do those who come from elsewhere where the winter does not seem to immobilise time and freeze the senses better perceive this photographic character of the snowed-in, frozen city? I do not know.

Beyond this confusing coincidence between Giorgia's developing photographic experiences and the actual essence of the city, these photographs marked the beginning of our friendship. They reveal also the continuation of a work of intimacy in which a poetic sense of the hidden is revealed: interior and exterior, visible and invisible, close and distant, here and elsewhere. In *Self Portrait* we imagine her, we look for her, we perceive the mass of her naked body in movement behind the blur of white soap suds, domestic snow that covers her like a second skin, light, vaporous, and fragile. At the photographic instant of time standing still her body in movement manifests itself against an unlimited black background. Her body hidden and revealed by the ephemeral suds becomes another body, another form, a body that escapes us, a ghostly body, as elusive and impalpable as the moving silhouettes disappearing at the corners of the snow-bound streets. Body-mirror of her own impressions.

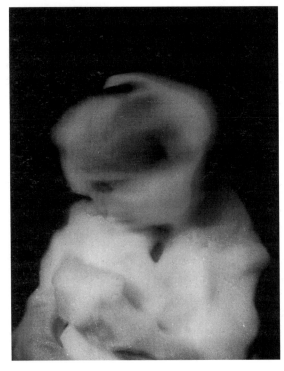

Giorgia Volpe:
Self Portrait (1998)
photograph
61 x 51cm (24 x 20in)

Other photographs of this same winter also offer images of intimacy in which we find this play between the visible and the invisible, this play of what remains unseen and hidden which leads us to reverie: in a dark room, a luminous source from behind an oval table filters through the veil of a white cotton table cloth and illuminates the floor softly. Like a nocturnal dream the light reveals a hiding place protected by the cloth. One imagines nestling into a bird's nest, warm and secret. The kitchen, the place of the smells of childhood, becomes by magic a shelter that protects the dreamer. In his book *La Poétique de l'espace*,[2] Bachelard shows how much the 'evocation of winter is a re-enforcement of the happiness of a home' and how much 'the attenuation of the outside world provokes an increase of intensity of all the intimate values'. All of Giorgia's winter photographs emanate this intensity. They are the work of a poet dreaming with her eyes open in this unknown city. A daydream that remains in the world, looking at terrestrial objects. A little text in prose, that she had written and gave to me suggests, like a precious collage of three Haïku poems, the other photographs of the series:

> It snows
> I walk, looking inside,
> In the windows.
>
> In the dark of the night,
> A transparent house, illuminated.
> From inside, somebody looks at me.
>
> The landscape imprinted on the mattress.
> A road that leads me
> somewhere …

On the photograph a mirror placed against the mattress reflects the linear motifs of the fabric to trace pathways that lead us to an unlimited elsewhere. This is a metaphoric image of travelling Giorgia, perpetual dweller of nomad territories, a bit like the snails who cross space carrying their homes on their backs and whose shells she likes to collect. Everyday reveries have no end and intimate spaces possess all their places of passage through which the imagination slips and memory awakes: in a reflection, a shadow, a trace, an old object, behind a window, a curtain, a table cloth, a veil, on a wall, a sheet, in the corner of an old, abandoned house. Furthermore, Giorgia entitles this series *Cahiers photographiques de passage*. I remember her speaking to me of a feeling of floating, detachment and immateriality during this period of acclimatisation and creating links with a new community. She was not yet settled. Her body was not yet anchored. It was the time of nocturnal wanderings, under the sign of the moon.

Between the Skins

Today I no longer perceive in her this sensation of not being completely here, this sense of being elsewhere, travelling. Her feet have taken root and her being no longer floats. She is here. Curiously, I see, with distance, that by becoming rooted she returns in her work to her research investigating organic forms, which she started in Brazil. We find again in her work the desire to allow the sense of sight to be guided by the sense of touch, the desire to pass from an internal and dream-like voyage to something that only addresses itself to the senses. In an attempt to sensualise the image, she reaches another imaginary approach. In an organic creative process, the photographic series *Plis*, which she created in Sao Paulo, led to the development of the project *Un Espace Trop Proche*[3] here in Quebec. By the juxtaposition of digital prints on all the walls and the floor, made from the photographs of folds of bodies, Giorgia invents another body assembled with many fragments. A new body, in perpetual formation in which, by this effect of skin on the surface of the space, by this curving line of the fold that hides and reveals, the visitor is invited to penetrate.

Giorgia takes the photograph out of the frame to create 'a body that clothes the space and makes of the space another body to live in'.[4] From this moment, the quest for a penetrable space impregnated with corporeality takes her from the photographic exploration to a textile installation entitled *Derrière le Rideau (Behind the Curtain)*.[5] Like an onionskin, it becomes the passage of a skin (the folds of a body enveloping in a perpetual metamorphosis) to another skin: the skin of black and white clothing, underwear, and veils cut out and re-sewn into a single curtain, pierced with holes.

Having passed through the curtain, the visitor penetrates an empty space, in which suspended by invisible threads there is a curtain of organs, visceral substitutes and body members of which the barely moving shadows projected onto the far wall form a third curtain, immaterial and impalpable (see colour plate 11). To slip *Derrière le Rideau* is to move between several skins, to physically feel the passage, to perceive the clothing like an extension of the body, the corporal envelope like a container opening and revealing its organs, the space like an envelope, like a piece of clothing, like a second skin.

Giorgia Volpe: **Derrière le Rideau (Behind the Curtain)** (2000)
installation, cloth, fabric, wax
9 x 4m (29 ¹/₂ x 13ft)

In her research of the *contact image*[6] and her work on perception, Giorgia naturally moved towards textile creation, which is characterised fundamentally by the border, border between the public and the private, the self and others, and the self and its surroundings. An art of textile, which renders all forms tactile and revives a sensorial memory because it can be touched, it has an odour, and keeps the memory of the gesture of the hands that have cut and sewn.

If the body constitutes the centre around which Giorgia's work grows, it is not the psychological body as sexual fantasy of Louise Bourgeois, neither is it the monstrous and grotesque body of Annette Messager, nor is it the tragic and disappeared body of Christian Boltanski (even if one can distinguish certain formal similarities between her work and theirs). Her body is one of the senses and memory. It would be more appropriate to make a link with the poetic sense of the Polish artist Magdalena Abakanowicz for whom it was essential to draw the spectator closer to her work through the tactile sense. Regarding her installations *Brown Coat* and *Black Environment* she said: 'I want one to penetrate into the folds and the slits of the tapestry as far as the interior where one can hide oneself. This contact must be as direct and natural as with a piece of clothing or the skin of an animal'.[7]

Under the Sign of Exu

In her exile, in this interval between two cultures, two worlds, two sensibilities, Giorgia upsets the borders and favours the between, that is the passage from one element to another. As if by slipping through this passage all is possible. Living in a new world, she works with the memory of the place where she no longer lives, Brazil. A crossbred memory, but from which an Afro-Brazilian identity and a sensibility emerges maybe even more. If her curtain of organs evokes directly for me the votive chapel *Nosso Senhor do Bomfim* in Salvador de Bahia where a multitude of wax limbs hang from the whole ceiling, the rest of her work and her way of being suggests above all to me a profound and unconscious memory of Candomblé, Macumba. This Afro-Brazilian religion is practised with the body, a body that becomes more than the body, because it is the place in which the slaves transported their gods, because it is the site of memory of their roots, rhythms and beliefs of their land of origin, the land of Africa, from which they were deported and dispossessed of all. A body in a state of trance into which the gods descend to counsel the mortal. And if Candomblé believes in the memory of the body, places and objects, it is also the dialogue with the Orixas, the pagan gods of whom Exu is the god of borders, the god of crossroads where the paths of men cross and where space opens into many directions. It is under the sign of Exu that Giorgia's work lies.

Exu of crossroads, Exu of exchanges, Exu of passages.

Let us continue our conversation.

Notes

1.   Centre of contemporary photographic production and diffusion in Quebec City.
2.   G. Bachelard, *La Poétique de l'espace*, p. 152.
3.   Exposition *Un Espace Trop Proche* à la galerie *L'Espace Virtuel* Chicoutimi, Canada, 2000.
4.   Giorgia Volpe, 1999.
5.   Exposition *Derrière le Rideau* in the University's Laval Gallery, Québec, Canada, 2000.
6.   Giorgia Volpe, 1999.
7.   *Magdalena Abakanowicz*, p. 123.

Bodies, Clothes, Skins:
A Conversation in Quebec

Giorgia Volpe and Mariette Bouillet

Giorgia Volpe: When you read your text to me, I saw myself in it, and yet I saw myself from a distance. It is strange to hear someone else talk about oneself. Through your voice, I became someone else. The whole time, you were saying that I was looking for 'the body' … I, myself, ask myself what is the body that I am looking for? I am always thinking about this…. This question of the body is always present. In which body do I dwell? Which body surrounds me? What is the distance between my body and another?

Mariette Bouillet: I understand that my text gives you the impression that it is not you, because it is a personal vision. That's normal. But at the same time, do you think that my interpretation of this passage from the photographic image (the *contact image* as you call it) in which action and the senses are always present, to a work with textiles in which all imagery becomes tactile, is justified? Do you find the art of textile revives a sensorial memory, because it can be touched, it has an odour, and keeps the memory of the gesture of the hands that have cut and sewn?

GV: I find that there is a relation between the photographic image and the textile creation. What links them is the notion of contact. In the photographic image there is a desire for contact, to get closer, to touch with the gaze, the material, the forms, surfaces, and light. The photographic image itself is the result of a contact. It is an imprint of memory. And the textile work is also the result of a contact that develops over time, as does the photographic image. Both of them reveal a tactile memory. I think that we all have an archaic memory of this gesture of weaving. The memory of our grandmothers who knitted and told us stories at the same time …

MB: And the contact of the textile image is also the contact of fabric as envelope, as a second skin.

GV: Yes, fabric is a kind of envelope like the skin…. The skin is like fabric. We need this envelope to live in our body to dwell in our body, a body in a space, a body in a place. This is what interests me with fabric: the fabric as envelope, as a second skin in which to live. Because the skin is also a house, you live in your house. You dress it, you live in it, and thus you exist. And before even working with fabric, this intuition, this idea of skin as an envelope, was always present in my work. In a way I have the impression that I pass through different skins to discover which body I am looking for in my work.

MB: Yes, the skin is present…. And the memory of the body is also there. I see it in your photographic work *Un Espace trop proche* in which imprints of the folds of bodies form a weaving of folds that envelope space and create another habitable, penetrable body. And in your recent work, *Derrière le Rideau*, you worked with used clothing that had already been worn by people and carried the imprints of their body.

GV: Yes, in a way this link is possible. I don't know why, but it's true that I like used thing, things with a memory, things with which I can dwell in their memory and imagine.

MB: Everything is to be imagined …

GV: When you work with a piece of clothing that has been worn, it is as if you take on the skin of another, you live in another skin; it is as if you explore another body, another memory, another identity. And in this contact with another body, I think that you question, you transform your own body, your own identity. It is this experience of contact that penetrates an intimate space and transforms one body into another body, at times familiar and strange, that I would like to share with others. In the same way as when you live in another place, a new place, you can have this feeling of the familiar and the strange, and this sensation of transforming oneself.

MB: Yes … Furthermore it is a feeling that we both experienced during our first winter here in Quebec city…. This feeling of floating, detachment and at the same time the heaviness of all these new layers of skin to protect us from this previously unknown cold. It is as if we had the physical experience, in this sensation of floating, in this sensation of having no roots, that, to live in our own body, one had to have already settled somewhere.

GV: Yes, when one is in transit, travelling, with no fixed address, it is as if our feet have no roots, and our head looks for points of reference, because it is surrounded by new stimulus. So, one begins to find one's place when one stops and one says to oneself, I want to build something here. I don't know. You, who have decided to renovate a house here, you must be experiencing?

MB: It's true that since I've been renovating this house, I feel much more anchored, much more here. I *live* here. It is as if through fixing/taming this house, I am finding another mentality, another way of doing things. I discovered that the house is a kind of mirror for a country ... it is the culture itself, the whole identity of a country that is reflected in the house. ... You understand that the structure is all made in wood because lumberjacks built it, that the house had to have big basements because of the winter ice and the spring thaw, that the walls were made of many thicknesses with many empty spaces in between to insulate against the cold.

GV: Like envelopes ... You construct to appropriate the space in which you live.

MB: This evokes to me this image of the nest of leaves that you made in Rome when you were travelling. Like a sort of migratory bird that, at a certain moment in her nomadism, felt the need to stop to build a little ephemeral home.... Whether one is travelling or settled, it seems to me that this almost instinctive reflex to reconstruct a home is always present.

GV: Yes, I was in Italy, travelling, with only a little bag. And in Rome I had the opportunity to make an installation in a small gallery. I had nothing to work with. The only thing that inspired me were the leaves that were falling from the trees. It was autumn. I even remember when the leaves came to me one night, at a bus stop. They were accumulating around my legs and I saw a long skirt in this pile of leaves. It was like a suit that covered me in the city, protecting and enveloping me.... So for a week I collected a multitude of leaves in a bag that I brought back to an empty room that I filled up to the edge of its only open window. Then I entered into the pile and was once again surrounded by the leaves and looking out. The space became an extension of my body like a dress I was donning.

MB: Like the bird's nest that takes on the form of the bird's body.... Already, without working directly with textile, there was this link between

Giorgia Volpe: **Nest** (1996)
installation, leaves, projection

the body, the home and clothing: clothing like a home and the home like clothing. But I would like to go back to used objects, found objects, like those dead leaves that came to you.... I find that here in Quebec the garage sales, the flea markets seem to me to be more than just places of buying and selling. Beyond commerce they become places to meet, and exchanges of everyday objects in which there is already a multiple Quebecois identity,

Francophone, Anglophone, native Indian: photographic portraits of families, marriages; clothing, hand-crocheted bedspreads, popular knickknacks, dictionaries, kitchen utensils, catholic artefacts, hockey and winter gear, English teapots, and tools. And it seems to me that you work here a lot with found things, whether clothes or objects. Is this an accident or is it linked with this reality of flea markets?

GV: There was always a found thing at the origin of my desire to create. A found object gives me an idea, a thought in movement that has not yet found its place. I have an intuition and I let myself be guided by this intuition up until I find something that will surprise me. Something at times familiar, intimate, and yet also strange. And *strange*, but not in the sense of bizarre nor monstrous, but different. You never know where you're going to end up with a found thing, but you are in movement, in transformation and metamorphosis. Moreover, I agree with you about the sense of identity that flea markets carry within them. When you go into one, it is as if you are penetrating the memory of the objects to discover that of the country. So you have a contact with the objects that situate you in the memory of this place. And at the same time in this contact it is as if you discover yourself. Because there are things that belong to the *other* and that are also familiar to *you*, some which relate to you and others not.... These objects, these found objects, are sometimes similar to apparitions and revelations.

MB: One night we were wandering and by accident we found a big tube of flexible metal in a demolition site, a sort of metal snake. It was a big deal to bring it back to your studio on foot. And then you didn't touch it for a long time before transforming it.

GV: Since I have felt more settled here, since I am less transitory, I have the impression of having gone beyond the need to register this passage in photographic notebooks, as in a diary, and beyond the desire to keep a trace of the ephemeral and the transitory sense of my situation. I have arrived at a need of the concrete of the object and place. And today, as you say in your text, *I am there*. I don't know if it is the country where I *will* live, but I live here now. And here, I need to dwell completely; I need to find objects, to collect them, to create links between these objects, to find a space to install them, to construct a space woven with these objects so that they become a home, a new envelope, and another skin. An intimate skin. Because I find the body is something intimate. The skin is beyond the entire frontier between your fragility, your intimate space and the space that surrounds you. So, skin is this, clothing is this, home is this, the place where you are this. You go inside of it and you can go out of it.... There is this movement of transformation of the contour of the form, the taking on of new forms.

MB: In fact, in what you say I see a very strong link, being drawn between the body and identity. A transformable body that coincides with a moving and changing identity. And in relation to this I would like to evoke what the African slaves went through when they were deported to Brazil. These totally uprooted beings kept their identity in their completely naked bodies: they kept the memory of their rhythms, the memory of their gods in their bodies. And through time, in this new world, in the syncretism and crossbreeding, this identity has changed, has transformed to become something else, to renew itself.

GV: What you are saying profoundly relates to my culture of origin where the body was and still is the site of resistance and survival of this crossbred identity. It is not the cult of the body, the cult of physical culture, but it is to be present, to be really there, it is to live in one's body, because when you have nothing else, it is the only thing that still belongs to you.... Finally, all that we have is our body ...

MB: It is maybe in the Candomblé, this Afro-Brazilian religion in which the believers let the spirits enter their bodies, that this link that joins body, memory and identity is most clearly expressed. Furthermore what do the words of this mother of the Saints of Rio evoke for you?

> 'Once you wear a shirt or a pair of shoes for a long time, the destiny of these objects unite with yours. Man shapes what he wears to his own image; it becomes part of him. He abandons part of himself to it.'

GV: I think that this woman has expressed a synthesis of what the body is and the relationship of the body with the world because she makes a link between the body and the memory of objects related to it.

People are both material body and will, spirit, that activate the body and all that is outside of them.... Objects become transfers of his memory, it is him that will animate them.... They are extensions of him. For example, a Brazilian friend offered these coloured ribbons knotted around our wrists to us. They carry the inscription *lembranças do nosso senhor do bonfim,* apparently, they are nothing more than little pieces of knotted fabric, yet each knot corresponds to a wish, a secret, something intimate, that will happen the moment that the knot will break.... One could say that this goes back to popular beliefs, to superstitions. But the force of this ribbon is not only the object itself, but also what one projects onto it, it is one's secrets, remembered and forgotten, that are deposited in each knot. Furthermore, as the ribbon disappears, it has already become a part of our body.

MB: This ribbon is also a whole weaving of time, between a future that is projected in the secret of the wish and a past, very old belief that crosses the generations and lives on in the present, as we still wear the ribbon today.

GV: This makes me think also of a text that you wrote in which you talk about a little spool of black thread that 'sews together the memory of people and things'. Through this single spool you evoked a real story of a German immigrant who settled in Montreal ...

MB: Yes, in this spool of black thread that I found by chance I saw a strong metaphor of the thread of memory that links people, their objects and their past. It is the thread of the story of a German immigrant family that lives in Montreal. The first member of this family that immigrated here transported in his suitcases a large amount of spools of thread that he found by accident in an abandoned warehouse at the end of the Second World War. And his children continue to sew to make a living with this same thread. It is the thread of memory, it is the thread of generations, and it is the thread of continuity.

GV: You say also elsewhere, 'I don't like objects, it is the memory of things that they bring to me that I like'. These words speak to me because of the intimate way I perceive objects and the body. I see also in your writing a sort of thread that weaves links between memory of objects and people found by accident. Maybe in this common sensibility we have found a ground of exchange. I ask myself if it is not linked to our common situation of living elsewhere than our countries of origin.

MB: It is a question for me also. In which sense does the condition of being far away bring us closer to where we come from? It seems to me that from a distance one is more sensitive towards seeing from the outside what we bring within our roots. It is the paradox of being closer by being distant.... It is the distance that is missing when one is there. And maybe in this situation one feels closer to the at times similar and different experience of other immigrants. Each exile recalls a story. Maybe you also live here with a memory of Brazil within you.

GV: Yes, even more than when I am there. It is a memory that I carry in my body. And I also question myself about the displacement of cultures, values, objects, and religions from one country to another ...

MB: It is the essential question of identity, that of crossbreeding or of ghettoisation, of transformation or of fossilisation, of living memory or of dead memory, of taking roots or of being perpetually uprooted.

GV: At the same time, to choose something to bring with one, when one leaves for elsewhere, is because one needs this trace, this close thing that brings a continuity of what one was before and a transformation of what one is. I ask myself if I am not reproducing this, a little bit, in my work. I use found objects and I envelope them in fabric that I sew and knot to construct a unity between fragments. It is the fabric, like skin that covers, that unifies and links. This state of displacement of familiar objects in another place, another situation, and this transformation play on the object as a whole and part of a whole. In this new place the transformed object becomes other and also transforms the place. At least this I what I was looking for.

MB: It is a transformation that is natural with contact with the foreigner.... The foreigner changes you and changes himself with your contact. It is the transformation, the moulding of the self and the other in the displacement of values and identities, in contact and experience.

GV: And it is in this transformation that you construct and deconstruct, you remember and you forget, you stitch and you unstitch, you leave a trace and you erase ...

MB: It is an identity in metamorphosis ...

GV: It is an experience that develops over time. Time to see, time to appropriate and time to incorporate. Time as spatial time that is the in-between, 'The thread of passage', to remember your own image.

MB: And this thread of time takes on unexpected directions, curves, labyrinths in spirals, but it is also knotted.... The first knot, it is the umbilical cord ... and for me these knots of the thread are accidents, chances, coincidences to which we are more or less sensitive. All these knots make up what we are; they are the knots of memory ...

GV: And these knots, they link and they separate at the same time. The thread of time is also there, in the weaving with this thread that one knots and one cuts to give birth to another form. The body is present in this weaving, in this continual gesture that sews and repeats itself until it creates an extension of itself that one later cuts.

MB: We are already ourselves, beings woven of cellular and muscular tissue.... In a way we could follow this metaphor spun by weaving. The weaving of the thread of our memory, of the thread of your work that folds and unfolds, of the thread of my writing that weaves links between things and people, of the thread of our relationships to the Other. It is perhaps this continual weaving of threads that go off in many directions each taking on different forms that create identity.

FORBIDDEN TOUCH: ANNE WILSON'S CLOTH

Alison Ferris

In a brilliant essay, 'From the Museum of Touch', Susan Stewart directs us to Marx who, in *Economic and Philosophic Manuscripts of 1844*, claimed that 'the forming of the five senses is a labour of the entire history of the world down to the present'. Stewart explains:

'In suggesting that the senses are a historical, that is human, accomplishment, Marx argued that the senses are not merely organs, used in responding to, and apprehending, the world, but that the senses are also a powerful source of material memories. Such memories are material in that the body carries them somatically – that is, they are registered in our consciousness, or in the case of repression, the unconscious knowledge, of our physical experiences'.[1]

Anne Wilson mines the limits of the body, its senses, memory and their links to the world. Using found and family linens and altering them with tiny delicate stitches of thread and human hair, her work does not foreground explicit representations of the body. Yet the visceral body is symbolically present. This body is implied in Wilson's work not only through the tactile materials of cloth and hair but also through the suggestion of touch: her work emphasizes physical engagement – hand sewing – in the making of her art. In this way, Wilson creates visual paradigms of touch, works that inspire handling or invite a caress, an aspect of her work that is just as important, when experiencing it, as sight. Wilson's work, that is, encourages physical as well as visual investigations.

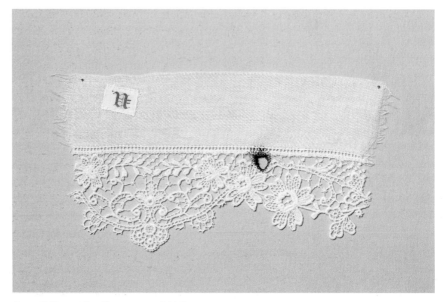

Anne Wilson: **Mendings, no. 3** (1995)
hair, thread, cloth
8 x 15cm (3 x 6in)

From the collars, cuffs, and dresser scarves in *Mendings* (1995) to her use of table linens in *Feast* (2000), Wilson has used primarily white cloth.

In *Feast*, the most recent and expansive work of this ten-year project, hundreds of excerpted holes from the wear in table linen are pinned onto a mammoth white-painted table. As Wilson herself has observed, 'this table, measuring 6.5 metres (22 feet) long and 1.5 metres (5^1/$_2$ feet) wide and .75 metre (2^1/$_2$ feet) high, is positioned diagonally, fills the gallery space. It is viewed intimately from the table edge. The holes and linear tears are the remnants from dining, residue / wear from the use-function of table linen; found objects, stitched open with human hair and fine thread. The holes have a connection to their origin through presentation horizontally on the table surface. The mammoth table and dining table height implicate a large social space; many diners, many interactions, many different histories of use.'

Wilson calls the work 'an abstract topography suggesting mapping and navigation, both internal and external to the body: pools, clusters, craters, mounds; fractals, particles; cellular-like; self-organised systems, blips and parts meandering as in a natural organism; displaced, interrupted, paired and split'.[2]

This approach thwarts fixed representation. By considering the relational aspects of position rather than the literalness of looking like anything fixed, the organisational logic of like-kinds take on another life; shape of hole or linear tear, hair colour, kind of cloth / of the same cloth in related proximity.

Wilson's white cloth also evokes skin. The link between skin and cloth is rich and varied and can be traced back to ancient times. Ewa Kuryluk investigates part of this history in her book *Veronica and Her Cloth: History, Symbolism, and Structure of a 'True' Image* where she explains that white cloth, in early Christianity, was 'the perfect material for visualising God's "clothing" in Mary's flesh'.[3] As an extension of early Christian associations of white cloth with that of the Virgin's immaculate body, white cloth is metaphorically associated with light, life and health, whereas darkness, mental obscurity, sickness and death are associated with dirty garments and rags. Kuryluk also observes that in depictions of the passion and crucifixion, skin and cloth and the paradoxical relation of one to the other is paramount. 'As skin dies', she writes, 'cloth may come alive and replace the body. When the body falls, garments fly up'.[4] Earlier even than the advent of Christianity, dead bodies were covered with shrouds of white linen to prevent corpses from disintegrating and, in turn, to provide the deceased with 'new dresses and skins'.[5]

White cloth is, then, associated with cleanliness, health and even vitality, yet, simultaneously, it is inextricably linked, by nature of its function, to the mortal, fragile body. Wilson's incorporation of hair into fine white cloths (tablecloths, handkerchiefs, and napkins) therefore suggests a domestic sphere that has failed, or a moral code infected with impurity. However, when Wilson accentuates holes and worn areas in the cloth / skin with stitching of thread and hair, it is by no means impossible to understand that the holes also allude to wounds, orifices, burns, disease or decay. In this manner, hair in Wilson's work refers in part to the abject body, the horror and repulsiveness of the fragmented body. Such work is now regarded as a melancholic return to the real, as current criticism has suggested about art created in the early 1990s when the body was frequently depicted as spectacle.[6] Yet in a way that distinguishes her from other artists, Wilson alludes to the body in a continuous process of becoming.

Although *Areas of Disrepair* (1993–7), *Grafts #1* and *#2* (1993), and *Mendings* employ different kinds of pristine white cloth, each of these series features holes that are 'disrepaired', to use Wilson's word. Wilson's references to holes, orifices or wounds are deliberately left ambiguous; in fact, their meaning rests on this ambiguity in a way that furthers the notion of transformation-in-progress. At the same time, however, the works appear to be in arrested development – plucked from whatever state they were in and isolated in small vitrines or cases for examination.

Lost (1998), Found (1998) and Misplaced (1998) are larger singular works, made up of considerable lengths of fabric that are delicately yet densely covered with hair (see colour plate 4). They suggest, like the specimens in Areas of Disrepair or Mendings, that there may have been more of this fabric and that we are seeing only a portion of it. The illusion Wilson creates is that there is no beginning or end to her works, that she has captured them in only one particular stage of their evolution. Had she not isolated them, we surmise, there may have been potential for further physical trans-formation.

These characteristics, combined with the exclusive use of white cloth accented with hair, bring us back again to flesh. The flesh, writes Amelia Jones, basing much of her observations on the writing of Merleau-Ponty, 'is a physical membrane that sheds and reconstitutes itself continually, the flesh is never always the same material but always a contour in process … metaphorically as well as materially, the flesh is an envelope, a limit inscribing the juncture between inside and outside but also a site of joining'.[7] One can argue, then, that in addition to representing the body in an ever-transforming state, Wilson's works inquire into the unlocatable limit between the body and the world, a limit always suggested and unsettled by skin.

Wilson's exploration sees tactile materials as transporting us to the thresholds of the body and the world, materials that do not merely represent physicality but rather embody it, possess it. And because of its highly tactile nature, Wilson's work invites experiencing with one's fingers as much as with one's eyes and mind. This fact, in and of itself, challenges the subject oriented, distancing vision typically associated with art. An object that references or invites physical handling or touch constitutes a particular way of knowing, which, according to Australian critic Sue Rowley, has intrinsic to it an articulation of a deeper, underlying critique of Enlightenment assumptions about knowledge, truth and rationality.[8] In other words, touch, or even the invitation to touch, is iconoclastic because it is the symbolic act that can breach the carefully constructed gap between the object (the physical) and the mind. The materiality of Wilson's work uses the notion of touch to offer an alternative to and critique of the intrinsic separation between body and mind that remains, to a large extent, intact in Western culture today.[9] Through Wilson's work, we can follow Stewart, who suggests that 'in searching for the relation between external and internal experiences of sense impression and in studying the historical manifestations of sense experience evident in works of art, we might find a way of approaching these questions that is more engaged with the dynamic between sense experience and thought than with their division'.[10]

A fine example of the dynamic between sense experience and thought is the making of textiles, problematically considered an art of the woman's hand, reinforced, in turn, by the tactile manner in which textiles themselves, namely clothing and bed linens, are utilised. By collapsing all of these links in her work, making skin and cloth one through meticulously obsessive stitching, Wilson actually examines how these many connotations associated with textiles do not necessarily add up. The intensity of the labour in each individual fragment of Wilson's work combined with the sheer number of these tiny works – not to mention the visceral effects caused by the hair – indicate an inherent contradiction. On the one hand, the labour involved in the stitching draws attention to the stereotype that collapses 'women' and 'patience', particularly when it comes to the production of textiles. On the other hand, the large quantity of these tiny works and the incorporation of hair suggest a transgressive breach of the tradition in sewing that emphasises restraint. Artist and textile historian Janis Jefferies elaborates on the recurring opposites of patience and deviation in relation to femininity and textiles:

'In Freud's writings, femininity is treated as supplementary, as parasitic to the masculine. What is at stake is the desire to repress that which negates or complicates the masculine position. Situated at the margin, the feminine is designated as a deviation, chaotic, wild and messy other whilst in another discourse it is also positioned as patient, prudent, and nurturing, representing the area of immersion in life, the natural part of a human being, the sphere of passivity and natural necessity. These two recurring oppositions amount to the two sides of the same male-ordered story, whether articulated in myth, history or metaphor.'[11]

Wilson's work metaphorically represents the unleashing of the repressed and requires us to turn our attention to this double encoding. Through her work, Wilson heightens our awareness regarding what Jefferies refers to as the 'veils of language' and how they have shaped the social, political and historical discourses in which textiles, as well as art made by women, are imagined and made.[12] In other words, Wilson brings all the paradoxes of women's work, including the inherent contradictions, into relief.

While qualities of femininity might be read in Wilson's process and technique, her work can by no means be understood as inherently feminine. In fact, the orifice-like holes in the cloths themselves could be regarded as disrupting the possibility of essentialism in that they work against any simple celebratory connotations of women and / or textiles. The holes, the visceral orifices, coupled with the way Wilson makes us think of textiles, ultimately lead us back to the juncture between the body (both male and female) and the world and in turn encourage the viewer to examine his or her own subjectivity and objectivity.

In fact, one might argue that this threshold, the boundary between the body and the world, is most visibly and viscerally represented in Wilson's work at the site of the body's orifices. Rather than simply emphasising orifices as dangerous and threatening to pollute, the orifices in Wilson's work also suggest the body's margins, a place of vulnerability especially because the orifices are the location on the body where the senses are concentrated and the most acute. The anthropologist Mary Douglas writes, 'all margins are dangerous. If they are pulled this way or that the shape of fundamental experience is altered. Any structure of ideas is vulnerable at its margins. We should expect the orifices of the body to symbolise its specifically vulnerable points'.[13] Susan Stewart writes that orifices subdivide our experience 'yet they are at the same time components of the body's general and synthesising openness to the world'.[14] Wilson's orifices can certainly be read as blurring the boundaries between culture and biology. In fact, Wilson further emphasises the margins of the body in her incorporation of orifice-like holes in clothing. For instance, in *Mendings* she makes tiny hairy holes in sections of collars and cuffs, details of clothing that function between the concealed, private body and the visibly public one.

Through the operation of the senses at the orifices, Stewart observes, we engage in an 'epistemology of process'.[15] The orifices in Wilson's work, therefore, bring us back to the senses and in Wilson's case, particularly to the notion of touch. Indeed, Wilson highlights our consciousness of touch using an age-old strategy, that of forbidding it. Wilson displays her work in such a manner, usually in deep shadow boxes or on shelf vitrines covered with plexi-glass, that prevent us from physically interacting with the work yet simultaneously beg our investigations of it. Her works function by the power of suggestion – they are not very different from that of an illusionist tease, which, one might argue ultimately, activates both the senses and the imagination. Marius Kwint, writing about the manner in which objects in the museum evoke touch, states, 'Although the prospect of touching an object is real, the desire to do so is suppressed, and so the imagination is forced to overcome the single sense to which art is usually delivered, by an almost synaesthetic process of evocation'.[16] This is not a manipulative tactic on Wilson's part, I might add, as many of us enjoy and deliberately seek such experiences, especially but not exclusively, when looking at art in museums. Objects can be found there that have the ability to unlock personal and collective memories, memories that are, as often as not, infused with imagination and desire. Appropriating formal museum display tactics, Wilson insures that her viewers have the same opportunity to locate their memories and desires in her work. This is to say, then, that the frustrated desire to touch her work inspires the viewer's own imaginative acts and memories.

However, objects in museums, unlike Wilson's work, are not isolated and protected in order to liberate memory but rather to insure their preservation. They become precious not only because they have been relegated to a museum but also because they must be conserved or maintained with care in order to survive. Stewart writes that objects held in museums 'store our labour, and our maintenance of them is a stay against the erosion of time'. She continues, 'Those works of art that we cannot touch are repositories of touch and care – the touch and care of their makers and conservators'.[17] Rather than keep this function of the museum squarely in the realm of institutional practices, Wilson, through her work, links the notion of preservation with that of touch. In so doing, Wilson makes visible the paradox upon which the survival of objects (as repositories of history and memory) rest – a desire to touch that must be suppressed and the touch of a caregiver.

A Chronicle of Days (1997–8) is one of Wilson's most ambitious undertakings, consisting of 100 works of altered white damask table linens, primarily napkins, created over the same number of days. Limiting herself to only one day to complete each work, she has stitched a spot or mark of hair and thread back into the patterned ground of the cloth. Wilson says, 'research in textile conservation labs has informed this work'. The archival framing, the cataloguing system, and the method of its visual display all serve, in Wilson's words 'to authenticate the objects as part of an historical record',[18] which is, then, a museum-like memorialisation.

Yet *A Chronicle of Days* is as much about process as it is about time. In fact, one might say that this work is about (borrowing art historian Richard Schiff's words) the 'physicality of historic events'. He observes that 'Like an artist's life, the objective conditions of history seem, retrospectively to have predetermined whatever acts have been committed, yet people's

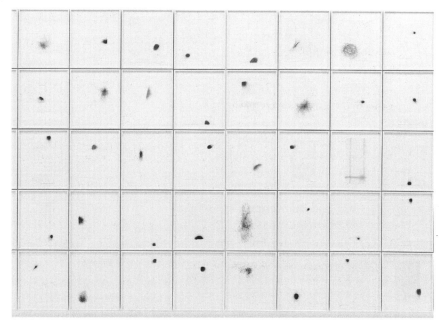

Anne Wilson: **A Chronicle of Days** (1997–8)
cloth, hair, thread, steel and glass frames
183 x 587cm (72 x 231in) overall

actions have given history its configuration'.[19] Therefore Wilson's work, emphasising touch not only in her use of tactile materials but also in the context of preservation, offers us another way to experience history, culture, the world. Touch is performed piecemeal (as opposed to vision which is panoramic) and through the metaphor of touch Wilson suggests that we can experience history and the world piecemeal and thereby create, perhaps, a tapestry of particularised memories in our own minds. Stewart writes, 'Just as memory enables us to distinguish our waking from our sleeping selves, so does touch cross the threshold between what is conscious and unconscious, what is passive and what is active, what is dead and what is living'.[20] Anne Wilson's tangible cloth, though small in scale, is expansive enough conceptually to carry these thresholds and, in turn, offers us the opportunity to conjure our own material memories.

Notes

1.   Stewart, 'From the Museum of Touch', pp. 17–18.
2.   Unpublished artist statement, June 2000.

3. Kuryluk, *Veronica and Her Cloth: History, Symbolism, and Structure of a 'True' Image*, p. 4.
4. Ibid. p. 197.
5. Ibid.
6. Grynsztejn, 'CI: 99/00', *Carnegie International 1999/2000*, p. 99.
7. Jones, Amelia, *Body Art: Performing the Subject*, p. 207.
8. Rowley, *Warping the Loom: Theoretical Frameworks for Craft Writing*, p. 182.
9. For elaboration on this point see Marcia Tucker, *A Labor of Love* (New York: The New Museum of Contemporary Art, 1996).
10. Stewart, op.cit. p. 18.
11. Jefferies, *Text and Textiles: Weaving Across the Borderlines*, p. 35.
12. I first wrote about this aspect of Wilson's work in the exhibition catalogue *Memorable Histories and Historic Memories*, Bowdoin College Museum of Art, 25 September – 6 December 1998.
13. Douglas, *Purity and Danger: An Analysis of Concepts of Pollution and Taboo* p. 121.
14. Stewart, p. 19.
15. Ibid.
16. Kwint, 'Introduction: The Physical Past', p. 6.
17. Stewart, p. 30.
18. Unpublished artist statement.
19. Schiff, *Cézanne's Physicality: The Politics of Touch*, p. 153.
20. Stewart, op. cit. p. 36.

THE SEWING DESIRE MACHINE

Peter Hobbs

The sewing needle is both prick and hole, it penetrates and is penetrated. If we lay two sewing needles side by side the doubling of pricks points to the doubling of holes. Anthropomorphism situates the eye of the needle in the anus. This brings to mind Georges Bataille's twin figures of the solar anus and the pineal eye.[1] For Bataille life is thoroughly parodic in that everything carries a trace of its opposite. This condition serves as an impetus that leads humans along signifying chains from one concept to the next. Bataille concludes from this that 'if the origin of things is not like the ground of the planet that seems to be the base, but like the circular movement that the planet describes around a mobile centre, then a car, a clock or a sewing machine could equally be accepted as the generating principle '.[2] Life, in other words, is not based on fixed structures, but is an active space of juxtaposition.

Art objects, with their heightened sense of connotation, perform a special role within this play of juxtaposition. They have the potential to push us in directions removed from the everyday. Art making involves actively pursuing connotative chains (this made me think of this, which made me think of this, which …). The connotations surrounding objects and ideas branch out and interconnect to form various discursive fields. In the following essay, the discursive field examined revolves around sewing and gay desire.

I have been recently drawn to sewing as a means of artistic expression. This was no doubt spawned in part by the attention that textile arts have received in the last decade in the world of contemporary art. It was also spawned by my interest in gay aesthetics. Sewing has provided me with a discursive field that I see as imbued with a gay or queer sensibility. Of course, I am not claiming that sewing is a gay activity, or an indication of one's sexual orientation. What I am claiming is just as simple: there are lines of thought that connect my activity as an artist and my identity as a gay man. Through sewing I have been pursuing what I have termed a queer needle. I want to discuss sewing in the context of a queer needle: how the sewing needle and machine are tools in the production of gay desire. However, sewing is not really the primary focus of this essay, but more of a metaphoric staging ground to discuss desire and aesthetics.

When I sit down in front of the sewing machine I am sitting down to what I see as a discursive machine already implicated in the production of gay desire. In my world, the sewing machine is first and foremost associated with women, and, as such, it has a certain queer potential. In addition to various speeds and stitches, my sewing machine has a gender bending option (see colour plate 7).

What I mean by this is that as a man by simply using a sewing machine my production is going to be understood as being outside social convention. In addition to its strong association with women (which I will pick up on later) the sewing machine can be seen as something of a queer machine, an agent of gay desire. In an attempt to clarify what I mean by this I will delineate some of the discourse surrounding sewing and the sewing machine and reference three artists that directly deal with ways that desire manifests. I do not mean to present this discourse as something free-floating that I just happened on. All discourse is ideologically charged, and what I want to do is, in effect, listen with a queer ear.

The sewing machine is featured in the simile coined by Lautréamont and often used as a descriptive of surrealism: 'Beautiful as the chance encounter of a sewing machine and an umbrella on an operating table'. This statement along with the inclusion of a sewing machine in Bataille's list of possible generating principles are examples of how the sewing machine functions as a cultural icon. Despite advancements in design and the integration of computer components, the sewing machine, like the electric hand drill or the electric iron, will always belong to a first generation of automated machines. Unlike more advanced forms of technology such as the radio, television, or computer, the mechanics of the sewing machine are readily apparent. Even if I cannot see all the working parts I am able to visualise them and their functions in my head. Nor has the sewing machine been threatened with obsolescence (how can one improve on the basic integration of a motor and a sewing needle?).

The sewing machine remains anachronistic in that it retains a sense of its human origins. Sitting in front of the sewing machine I can see the extent of my actions, which gives me the feeling of being incorporated into the machinery. In this respect, the sewing machine and its operator can be

Peter Hobbs: **Masturbation Blanket** (2000), from **The Secret of the Old Mill**
mixed media installation
160 x 140cm (63 x 55in)

thought of as something of a machine-human hybrid or automaton. A great deal of art from the first part of the twentieth century was fascinated with the integration of humans and machines. Automaton figures appear in many of the works of the futurists, the Dadaists, and the surrealists. Numerous examples include collages of both Max Ernst and John Heartfield that often featured figures made up of human and machine parts, Marcel Duchamp's use of images of funnels, grinders, and wheels in his 'bride and bachelor' portraits, and Hans Bellmer's photographs of female mannequins arranged in grotesque combinations. This work is part of an overall cultural obsession with machines. Inherent to machines is the idea of human obsolescence, or, at the very least, an evolutionary fantasy of human-machine integration. The introduction of the computer shifted the focus of this fantasy from automatons to that of cyborgs.

One of the predominant associations I make with the sewing machine is that it belongs to the domestic sphere. Like many middle-class families, the sewing machine was a feature of our suburban home. To cut costs, my mother sewed clothes, sheets, and curtains. She also knitted sweaters and did needlepoint samplers. Although my mother sometimes became bored with this activity, she also saw it as providing an ongoing creative outlet.

Been part of life since older generations

As must be the case for many individuals, my mother and her role as a housewife served as my first source of creativity. I remember my mother teaching my sister how to sew and knit, and my brothers and I periodically sitting down in front of the sewing machine and trying it out. I do not know if my mother feared that she would turn her boys into sissies if she was as diligent showing us sewing as she was my sister, but this stigma was certainly present.

To establish a gay context for the sewing needle it makes sense to look at the activities in which men have traditionally sewn. A brief list can be drawn from recent Western history that includes such individuals as tailors, fashion designers, interior decorators, prop and costume makers, prisoners and sailors.[3] This list could double for one representing the clichéd roles historically associated with gay men. The stigma of the queer needle is based on the idea that sewing has long been perceived as 'women's work', and such work is not valued in relationship to masculine pursuits. The rationale runs as follows: sewing is seen as being feminine; men who sew are unmanly; men who are unmanly are feminine; feminine men are queer.

In *The Subversive Stitch*, Rozsika Parker points out that the idea that needlework is feminine is in part the product of the Victorian period. She writes, '[The] Victorians presented the link between embroidery and women as entirely natural, thus concealing the complex social, political and economic factors that had connected the two since the middle ages'.[4] Promoting this perception was a way of furthering the notion that women find themselves in the domestic sphere – as wives, mothers and caretakers – as a circumstance of nature.

Alongside this notion that needlework is feminine is that it has also long been viewed in contrast to fine art as a craft. The hierarchical pairings – male/female, masculine/feminine, fine art/craft, and high art/popular arts – pile up and reinforce one another according to the tautological principle that is patriarchy.

With their combined associations with childhood, maternal care and domesticity, the needle and the sewing machine are machines producing both a sense of comfort and loss. This is related to what the child psychologist D.W. Winnicott refers to as 'transitional objects'. These are the blankets, pillows or stuffed toys that take on a 'special value for the suckling and young child, particularly when it is on the point of falling asleep'.[5] The child comes to rely on these objects as a means of coming to terms with the idea that he or she is separate from the mother. The distance that opens up between the mother and child 'provides the space necessary for creative potential'.[6] As such, even the most seemingly insignificant

Peter Hobbs: **Camp Blanket, Wilde Pillow** and **Warhol Pillow** (2000),
from **The Secret of the Old Mill**
mixed media installation
140 x 130cm (55 x 51in), 50 x 55 x 20cm (20 x 22 x 8in) and 60 x 65 x 20cm (24 x 26 x 8in)

looking textiles can be charged with a tremendous sense of time and meaning.

American artist Mike Kelley has capitalised on transitional objects and the feelings that they generate. The predominant concept of childhood is one of happiness and innocence. However, when it is reconsidered in terms of vulnerability and social taboos, the discomfort of childhood must also be acknowledged. The fact that childhood is a tremendous source of cultural anxiety registers in Kelley's art. He has used appliquéd blankets, stuffed toys and juvenile imagery to create an aesthetic of juvenilia that conflates childhood, sexuality and faeces. In doing so he has drawn a connection between transitional objects and the transgressive or taboo.[7]

In the mid-1980s Kelley began showing arrangements of handy-craft items culled from thrift shops. His *More Love Hours Than Can Ever Be Repaid* (1987) is a collection of stuffed animals and Afghans sewn together on a canvas backing to form a profuse mosaic. These rescued items may have served in various economies of emotional investment, as both transitional objects and markers of love. Economies, including emotional ones, work on a principle of exchange organised according to supply and demand. As such, they can become bankrupt if presented with a deficiency or excessiveness. Love in the form of expressed sentiment has long been seen as bankrupt. Added to this dilemma is that, in relationships of love and care giving, the involved parties can often feel cheated, that their investments were never reciprocated in kind. As stated in the piece's title, the sheer volume of blankets and stuffed toys that Kelley presents us with suggests an emotional economy that has over-extended itself and gone awry.[8]

As in birth and childhood, textiles also serve as transitional objects in the psychology of death. The figure of the deathbed, along with the idea that we will all eventually succumb to an eternal sleep, infuses blankets and pillows with connotations of death and illness. In some cultures this chain of association also includes the burial shroud. It is also through the bed, as well as clothing, that textiles are associated with sex. The bed is the primary site of fundamental human experience: birth, sex, and death. As such, the bed and the bedroom are motifs featured throughout art history. This idea of the bed as an agency of primary experience is part of the strength of *The Names Project* (or the *AIDS Quilt* as it is better known).

The *AIDS Quilt* was inaugurated in 1987 in Washington D.C., at which point it was equivalent in size to two football fields. Subsequently, the quilt has doubled several times in size. '[It] has been exhibited throughout the world and includes more than 40,000 panels from twenty-nine countries, yet it represents a mere fraction of those who have died from AIDS'.[9] Operating on different levels of experience and involvement, the quilt is a powerful piece of communal art. It provides a form of mourning that can be felt both directly and indirectly.

While one might react to the quilt on a personal level, it has provided a way to establish a community of experience, as any one name or panel in the quilt is read in terms of the whole. It also functions as an effective form of political protest. In its ever-increasing size the quilt has obvious political implications that are difficult to ignore.

AIDS has claimed the lives of many artists, including Cuban born Felix Gonzalez-Torres, who died in 1996. Gonzalez-Torres lived in New York City where he was a member of the collective Group Material. The collective was formed in 1979, but was most active in the late eighties. Along with Gonzalez-Torres, it consisted of Tim Rollins, Julie Ault, and Doug Ashford. They put on a number of exhibitions dealing with different social issues in which they adopted strategies with a democratic emphasis. These included soliciting objects and art from artists and non-artists to be shown together, and organising public discussions to coincide with their exhibitions. In 1989 they exhibited *AIDS Timeline* at the University Museum in Berkeley, California, which consisted of a mixture of solicited artworks, personal objects, medical reports, video clips, magazines and posters, all of which was hung in clusters along a timeline. This show was similar to that of the *AIDS Quilt* in that the epidemic is placed in a historical and personal context.

In comparison to the straightforward approach of Group Material, Gonzalez-Torres' solo work is based on poetic metaphor. Certain objects and motifs repeat throughout his career, including curtains, mirrors, piles of candy, stacks of paper, strings of lights and the use of particular colours. These elements are used in a sparse manner that echoes minimalism. His paper stacks and his candy spills are a direct reference to the work of Carl André and Robert Smithson. But where these artists worked with minimal elements as a means to strip their work of external references and a sense of authorship, Gonzalez-Torres allows for compassion and biographical import. For example, the shimmering silver carpet of candies that comprises Gonzalez-Torres' piece *Untitled (Placebo)* (1991) represents the combined weight of the artist and his lover Ross, who died of AIDS in 1991. The viewer is meant to interact with the work by taking a piece of candy and sucking on it, thereby, symbolically consuming the couple's bodies. This act of communion is much different from the detached experience of the body akin to minimalism. I may become aware of my body when viewing a Minimalist piece, but this remains an exercise in physics that has nothing to do with personal experience. The body that Gonzalez-Torres evokes is situated in the real world. It is a living body that I hold in my mouth, one with a tangible sense of personal history.

Gonzales-Torres also evoked feelings of loss by exhibiting sheer, blue curtains. These curtains have appeared on a number of occasions in different lengths and arrangements. Viewed hanging in front of a window, the curtains cast a blue glow and are sometimes shown billowing in the breeze, leading one to imagine a tempered apparition or recall a fleeting memory. This ephemeral gesture is typical of Gonzales-Torres' work – it is bold in its simplicity.

The American artist Jim Hodges works in a similar manner to that of Gonzalez-Torres. He too uses found objects and arranges them in such a way that they speak volumes about human experience, or, more specifically, his experiences as a gay man. His work is also heavily laden with allusions to mortality and mourning. *Landscape* (1998) consists of a man's white dress shirt stuffed with layers of other dress shirts. The dress shirts incrementally decrease in size all the way down to that which would fit a small child. As one might look at a tree stump and count the rings, the viewer looks down the collar of the white dress shirt, sees diminishing rings of different colours and patterns and in this way is presented with an effective marker of temporality.

Hodges has also created a number of curtains or scrims made from silk flowers. A great deal of repetitive labour went into the making of such pieces as *In Blue* (1996) and *You* (1997). Each of the curtains contains numerous silk flowers that have been rounded up, detached from their fake stems, ironed flat and then embroidered together. In their large scale and use of rich colours they appeal to the viewer on a sensual level. The obvious artificiality of the curtains runs contrary to the prevailing notion of beauty (being the result of a discerning judgement that avoids using material that is considered 'common' or 'tacky'). Here the aesthetics of craft and camp usurp the position traditionally reserved for high art.

I want to further stress that the return to formalism and beauty present in the work of Gonzalez-Torres and Hodges involves a critique of these concepts. In an interview with Tim Rollins, Gonzalez-Torres reiterates the point that politics affect how and what we see and interpret as art. He states, '[After] twenty years of feminist discourse and feminist theory we have come to realise the "just looking" is not *just* looking but that *looking* is invested with identity: gender, socio-economic status, race, sexual orientation.... Looking is invested with lots of other texts.'[10] Similarly,

Hodges has spoken about a need to redefine beauty in the context of his own life. In an interview he states 'It was very important that I own [beauty] for myself.... So I set out to understand what the word meant to me'.[11]

Both Gonzalez-Torres' and Hodges' work is extremely visually appealing. They would run the risk of simply being purveyors of 'eye candy' if the beauty generated by the work was not grounded in personal experience. Gonzalez-Torres and Hodges use beauty in such a way that causes the viewer to identify with these experiences. This does away with the notion that beauty and desire are timeless or universal truths, and replaces it with the idea that different people have different desires and notions of beauty related to who they are. In other words, Gonzalez-Torres and Hodges situate desire and beauty within a cultural context.

Two modern philosophers of desire, Gilles Deleuze and Felix Guattari, shape the notion of desire focused on in this essay. Writing as a team, Deleuze and Guattari conceive desire not as an aggregated entity that arises solely out of our unconscious or conscious will, but as a fractured form of energy that is generated in the mechanics of human interaction. Desire is not to be thought of as a by-product of the oedipal complex, as it is in Freudian psychoanalysis, but as a product of multiple actions and reactions. Deleuze and Guattari refer to the functions of the human body and the external forces with which it interacts as multiple machines. 'Everywhere *it* is machines – real ones, not figurative ones: machines driving other machines.... An organ-machine is plugged into an energy-source-machine: the one produces a flow that the other interrupts. The breast is a machine that produces milk, and the mouth a machine coupled to it.... Hence we are all handymen: each with his little machines'.[12]

Deleuze and Guattari depict the agency of desire also as a series of machines operating on the level of fragments. '[It] does not take as its object persons or things, but the entire surroundings that it traverses, the vibration and flows of every sort to which it is joined, introducing therein breaks and captures – an always nomadic and migrant desire'.[13]

In their writings, Deleuze and Guattari emphasise production over representation. They reject Freud's idea of the oedipal complex as it presents desire as a representation of the 'lack' we incur as infants because our oedipal fantasies are thwarted. As a replacement to psychoanalysis they propose what they term 'schizoanalysis'. Where the former employs the idea of 'territorialism', where we fit or do not in regards to the oedipal triangle, the latter employs a 'deterritorialism', or what Deleuze and Guattari call 'nomadic thought'. This is an agency unhindered by the guilt and remorse suffered by the Freudian subject, whose desires only ever manifest in a sublimated form. Deleuze and Guattari advocate a form of desire that is Nietzschian in that it operates beyond imposed notions of good and evil.

In a different context, the American art critic Dave Hickey also favours production over representation. In his text *The Invisible Dragon* he distinguishes images that 'do things' from images that 'only do things after we have talked about them'. Hickey is not advocating a notion of blind faith, but a corrective form of vision. 'If our criticism aspires to anything beyond soft-science, the efficacy of images must be the cause of criticism, and not its consequence – the subject of criticism and not its object'.[14]

I believe that in the work of Kelley, Gonzalez-Torres and Hodges there is, to different degrees, also an emphasis on production rather than representation. These three artists add to the discourse of desire by fabricating 'desiring machines'. This is the result of their work not only referencing the body, but also infusing the viewer with a tremendous feeling of embodiment, that can be best defined as being a mixture of uneasiness and longing. In all three cases this has involved the use of transitional objects. Whereas Kelley employs the transitional objects of infancy, Gonzalez-Torres and Hodges use those associated with death and mourning. And whereas Kelley engages in a playful aesthetic that bridges both juvenilia and abjection, Gonzalez-Torres and Hodges engage in a rehabilitated form of Minimalism, one instilled with a strong sense of personal loss.

What I have tried to establish in this essay is part of the context that I plug into when I plug in my sewing machine. At times this contextual frame may seem disparate and tangential, which brings us back to Bataille's idea that thought is a play of like and dislike. What I have attempted to do is articulate some of the thoughts that buzz around my sewing machine and resound in my queer ears. The idea is that by pursuing these different lines of thought, in which desire and sewing are linked, my sewing machine will also function as a desiring machine.

Notes

1. See Georges Bataille, *Visions of Excess: Selected Writings 1927–1939* (Minneapolis, University of Minnesota Press, 1985).
2. Ibid. p. 5.
3. I came across two interesting essays that discuss the relationship between embroidery and tattooing evident in the history of sailors: Matthew Benedict, 'Tattoo – Embroidery: the Text of the Law Upon the Body', *The Chicago Art Journal* (1992), and Robin Metcalfe,

'Queer Stigmata: The Embroidery Art of Robert Windrum', *Material Matters* (Toronto: YYZ Books, 1998).

4. Rozsika Parker, *Subversive Stitch: Embroidery and Making of the Feminine* (London: The Women's Press Limited, 1984), p. 189.

5. J. Laplanche, and J.B. Pontalis, *The Language of Psycho-Analysis* (New York: W. W. Norton & Company, 1973), p. 464.

6. Neil S. MacInnis 'At a Safe Distance: Textile as Transitional Object', in *The City Within*, ed. Jeanne Randolph (Banff, Alberta: Banff Centre for the Arts, 1992), p. 47.

7. Similarly, Mary Kelly, another American artist, has shown transitional objects in the form of her infant son's soiled diapers as part of a piece on motherhood entitled *Post-Partum Document*.

8. For a thorough examination of Kelley's prolific career, see John C. Welchman's survey essay 'The Mike Kelley's', *Mike Kelley* (London: Phaidon Press Limited, 1999).

9. Marita Sturken, *Tangled Memories: The Vietnam War, the AIDS Epidemic, and the Politics of Remembering* (Berkeley: University of California, 1997), p. 183.

10. Felix Gonzalez-Torres interview by Tim Rollins, *Felix Gonzalez-Torres* (New York: A.R.T. Press, 1993), p. 21.

11. Jim Hodges interviewed by Gean Moreno, *New Art Examiner*, June 2000, p. 14.

12. Gilles Deleuze and Felix Guattari, *Anti-Oedipus: Capitalism and Schizophrenia* (Minneapolis: University of Minnesota Press, 1992), p. 1.

13. Ibid. p. 292.

14. Dave Hickey, *Invisible Dragon* (Los Angeles: Art issues. Press, 1993), p. 12.

Voyage: Home is Where We Start From[1]

Kay Lawrence and Lindsay Obermeyer

Preface

Kay Lawrence and Lindsay Obermeyer met in March 1999 at the *Close Ties* Conference, which was held at the University of Queensland in Brisbane, Australia. It was in this context of exploring ideas of contemporary theory and their potential for negotiating the space between textiles and contemporary art that each artist presented a paper on her practice. Kay and Lindsay's common interest in using the medium of textiles to explore questions of identity, which arise from the relationship between mothers and daughters, led them to begin this correspondence.

> 'Severed from the placenta and cast from the womb, we enter the world as an amputated body whose being will be determined by the very mortality of that body'.[2]

The question of loss is central to the experience of subjectivity. This cycle of loss begins with our separation from the body of the mother and ends in death. But birth also connects us to the world. This is where we begin the process of negotiation between our inner world and outside reality through which the self develops.

As we construct our selves through the processes of making and through language, the very words we use to describe ourselves – woman, daughter, mother, friend, artist – speak of the fluidity of identity. Even a category as seemingly fixed as 'gender' proves to be mutable in human development.

Kay:

When I found some tiny drawings my daughter had made when she was six, of bodies with both male and female genitals, I became intrigued by the question of how we develop a sense of gender identity. My translation of her drawings into woven tapestry in the work *Gender Tapestry* made in 1993, links the child's understanding of gender difference to the loss of a sense of oneness with the mother, to the loss of 'Mother' as a sign for plenitude and completeness.[3] When the loss of the mother is physically experienced at a young age, the construction of identity and feeling of connection to the world can unravel. This loss is heightened when a nurturing adult does not step in to fulfil the role of 'Mother'.

Lindsay:

  My daughter had experienced the loss of two mothers by the time she was seven years old. During our first few years together, she needed me next to her during all waking hours in our apartment. To help alleviate her anxiety about separation, I knitted a sweater with sleeves fifteen feet long

Kay Lawrence: **Gender Tapestry** (1993)
woven tapestry
39 x 157cm (15 x 62in)

that connected us to each other. I could go into another room, close the door, and with a tug of the sleeve, I reassured my daughter of my presence (see colour plate 16). In the healing of her pain from the loss of two mothers, my daughter was simultaneously bonding with and separating from me. This process of both mending and loosening the bond between mother and child repeats itself throughout the life of both until death creates the final separation. The enduring connection of textiles to the body offers rich metaphorical possibilities for exploring this idea of identity as we attempt to integrate our inner psychic reality with the outside world and make sense of the experience of living.

Voyage

Voyage involves miles of travel – physical and psychological. Our words float over airwaves from satellite to satellite and into our respective faxes and computers. As letters, our words literally travel over land and water by plane or boat. To manoeuvre my daughter through her mental illness is to embark on another voyage while your time travel to the past to make sense of the present is yet another.

Lindsay Obermeyer: **Connection** (1998)
two hand-knit, mohair sweaters connected by 15ft sleeves, worn by artist and daughter

Kay, 10 September 1999:

While you work with your daughter, I work with images my daughter Ellie has made or photographs I've taken of her. She is now aged 21. There was a time lag of many years between making the images and using them, so my work seems to be more about making sense of the past, my own past through my relationship with her.

I wonder if you've heard of the Australian writer Drusilla Modjeska? She has been in the media frequently these last weeks talking about her new book *Stravinsky's Lunch*,[4] a history, but also a discussion about the demands of life and art in relation to the work of two Australian painters, Stella Bowen and Grace Cossington Smith,[5] both born in the 1890s. I was struck by something she said in an interview on the radio this morning about the relationship of creativity to children's play. She talked about Winnicott's notion of 'transitional space'[6] as that place where the child, confident in the mother's presence, feels free to explore. It's a place that is secure but unbounded so the child feels free to take risks. Re-reading Winnicott, it seems that it is the mother's reliable presence that can create this first space of interplay between the child's internal psychic reality and the external world, an interplay that forms the basis of creative living.

Modjeska believes that creativity requires the security of being held, accompanied by a sense of boundless possibility. She raised the question of how these conditions can be met in an artist's life. It seemed in her discussion that this 'holding' involved both external and internal factors, Virginia Woolf's room of one's own[7] and an income of £500 a year, but also the ability to 'hold' one's self, to have some sort of inner security and conviction.

I began to think back to the birth of my first child Toby, this day in fact 24 years ago. His birth marked that point in my life when I knew I had to make time for my own work or abandon all thought of becoming an artist. I'd always thought that it was the realisation that my time was not my own any more that focused me. But reflecting on this idea of being held, I had the sudden insight that perhaps it was his birth that tethered me, and held me (and constrained me as well of course).

Perhaps for me, feeling connected, in that fundamental way that having a child connects you to the world, was the 'holding' that enabled me to pick up my practice again. But I picked up textiles rather than painting.

It's only now that I understand this choice. It was the connection between the processes of weaving and the rhythms of the body that drew me in: a contemplative quality in the practice of weaving that enables the mind to run free while your hands are engaged, a form of practice that encourages

Plate 1
Sliman Mansour: The Village Awakens (1990)
oil on canvas
120 x 80cm (47 x 31^1/$_2$in)

Plate 2
Nalini Malani: Remembering Toba Tek Singh (1998), detail
video installation

Plate 3
Mayan Weaver (1985)
backstrap weaver brocading panel for *huipil.*
San Antonio Aguas Calientes, Guatemala

Plate 4
Anne Wilson: Lost (1998)
Hair, thread, cloth, leather cord, wood chair
91 x 56 x 60cm (36 x 22 x 23^1/$_2$in)

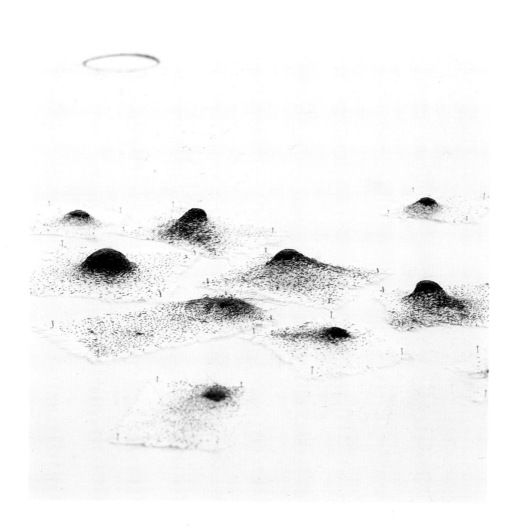

Plate 5
Anne Wilson: Feast (2000), detail
Hair, thread, cloth, pins, wood table
80 x 168 x 671cm (31$^1/_2$ x 66 x 264in)

Plate 6
Greg Leong: Australian (Red) – My Mother's Bridal Ensemble (1999)
silk brocade, Thai silk, lace fused on polyester satin, screen-print,
metallic thread, polyester satin
jacket: 88 x 138cm (35 x 54in), skirt: 88 x 99cm (35 x 39in)

Plate 7
Peter Hobbs: Travelling Gay Circus: The Secret of the Old Mill (2000)
mixed media installation
4 x 4.6 x 9m (13 x 15 x 29ft)

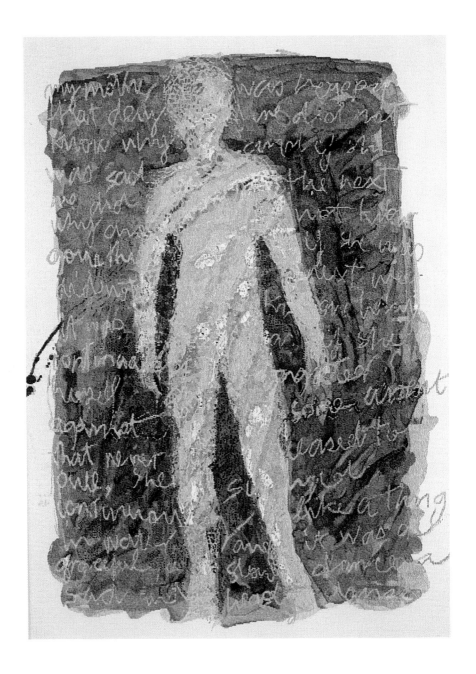

Plate 8
Kay Lawrence: Daughter (1995–96)
woven tapestry
195 x 142cm (77 x 56in)

Plate 9
Kim Sooja: Bottari (1995)
used clothes and bedcovers; Yongyou Island

Plate 10
Kim Sooja: A Needle Woman (1999)
video still from a performance in Shanghai

Plate 11
Giorgia Volpe: Derrière le Rideau (Behind the Curtain) (2000)
installation with cloth, fabric, wax
9 x 4m (29$^1/_2$ x 13ft)

Plate 12
Elsa Agelii: Wilderness (1997)
embroidery inspired by *Women who Run
with the Wolves* by Clarissa Pinkola-Estés
170 x 170cm (67 x 67in)

Plate 13
Glynis Humphrey: Gorge (1996)
voile, tulle, crinoline, polyester, cotton, canvas,
pencil rod, chicken and grid wire, clamps,
pinning devices, steel tension wire
460 x 275cm (15 x 9ft) (Women's dress size 66)

Plate 14
Cathy Daley: Untitled (1996)
pastel on vellum
231 x 107cm (91 x 42in)

Plate 15
Jenny Hansen: Blue Poppies (1998)
tapestry, hand-dyed wool on cotton
2 x 2.5m (6^1/$_2$ x 8ft)

Plate 16
Lindsay Obermeyer: Connection (1998)
two hand-knit, mohair sweaters connected by
15ft sleeves, worn by artist and daughter

reflection. When Jasleen Dhamija[8] likened the rhythms of weaving to the rhythms of breathing I knew why I wove. It's the still point in my life.

It's like a form of meditation. Paradoxically of course it's intellectually very demanding. Perhaps it's these very contradictions that I need. The processes of weaving are intrinsically related to the ideas embodied in my work, which during the last ten years have dealt with the subject of loss.

With the tapestry *Daughter* that I wove during '95 and '96, I was trying to understand and articulate my sense of loss over my mother's death when I was in my early twenties, and my realisation of the gulf of incomprehension that separates the child from the parent. I am now older than my mother was when she died. I think about her life and have insights into her experience that were unavailable to me when I was younger. I realised when I was weaving this image that in this work I occupy the space

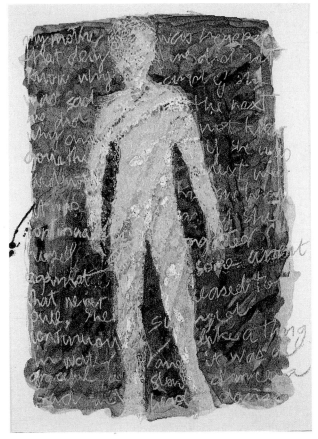

Kay Lawrence:
Daughter (1995/96)
woven tapestry
195 x 142cm (77 x 56in)

of both mother and daughter. Now that my own daughter has reached adulthood, I am coming to terms with the inevitability of loss between mothers and daughters, not only loss by death, but the separation that accompanies independence.

The process of weaving *Daughter* was a form of reparation for me. Weaving the words, building up the image, creating a dense physical structure and making good the damage of the past. The slowness of its making created a place for thinking and reflection, enabling me to return to my past and to repair a little of the anguish of that early loss.

In the discussion of your work at the *Close Ties* Forum, you mentioned your daughter's fear of being left. A very rational response I would have thought from a child like Emilie who has suffered so many losses, the loss of her natural parents, her country, her language. The sweater with the fifteen-foot sleeves that joined her to you seemed in a way to test the limits of Winnicott's transitional space. The images of you both running in the park in that absurd garment that should have been confining but enabled her to roam while secured to you, made visible the sort of 'holding' that Modjeska was discussing.

I remember you saying how you enjoyed making the piece. How it fitted in with your life as a mother, shop keeper, teacher, knitting the parts of your life together as much as knitting a garment.

Listening to the radio a month or so ago, I heard a woman describe how she kept despair at bay by knitting bedspreads. Her young, teenage foster son was on drugs. There seemed to be no institutional support to help her. When the interviewer asked her how she coped, she just said, 'I knit'.

Lindsay, 16 September 1999:

I deeply appreciated the story you wrote about the foster mother who said 'I knit'. One could tweak Descartes' famous dictum, 'I think, therefore I am'[9] to 'I knit, therefore I am'. It is the meditative quality of the textile arts that draws me to them. The thinking is arduous as you said, but after a certain point my mind lets go. I am always surprised by how time has passed while knitting. I move into a space where I just am.

Buddha called the components of personality *skandas*, which translates as skeins. Memory is what connects the grown adult to the child. As one grows and changes, the loops of Self are continuously connecting with each other through memory. As I knit loop into loop my memories intersect and connect to my present Self.[10] By letting go of abstract reasoning and letting my mind float as I work, I am able to gain a clearer insight into what I am trying to say. I get a clearer sense of my present Self.[11]

The process of knitting isn't about clearing my mind to a blank nothingness, but connecting to an everything. 'Is' is to be – to exist, to live connected to others, both my former Selves and other people.

Kay, 24 September 1999:

I was saddened to hear about Emilie's mental illness. I realise that my image of Emilie is the happy-go-lucky child of the photographs. My daughter during a difficult time in her own adolescence cut the skin of her inner arm. I was shocked to the core. Fortunately, the stresses that troubled her eased and she never did it again. But I felt compelled to make a series of drawings so I could come to terms with the experience.

While Ellie readily agreed to my photographing and drawing the marks on her arm, I never felt entirely comfortable about exhibiting the drawings even though they were not specific and didn't identify her. I only showed them once. Their value for me was in the process of making them and not in their public exhibition.

But it's a tricky situation when you work with material based on someone else's life, particularly a daughter whose life is enmeshed with yours but who needs to conceive of herself as separate in order to develop her own identity. My investigation of Ellie's experience to explore aspects of my own identity blurred those boundaries in my mind if not in hers. Which maybe is why I needed to work with material from the past not the present.

Lindsay, 15 October 1999:

The season is changing to fall now. It seems a bit odd, as I have already experienced fall this year. When we met in March, Brisbane was so warm and hot, not at all like the cool weather here. The smell, the feel of the air let me know that change was coming. And perhaps it was the pumpkins. Pumpkins I think were created to remind one of fall. Jack-o-lanterns and pumpkin pie. In Brisbane I indulged in numerous pumpkin delicacies, which I am now trying to recreate, such as pumpkin scones and pumpkin ravioli. Is it because touch and smell are a part of the brain stem that these senses become so critical in creating clear memories?

Fall is my new year. I was born on November 6th. This is the time I reflect upon my year and consider changes and plans for the future. I am struggling to find the balance. I've been reading the journals kept by the artist Anne Truitt. A voice older than my own speaks to me. I am seeking advice on how to steady myself for a major life shift by looking at how others have lived. Truitt wrote in 1991:

I think … of how the life I live in my house has been factored into the life I live in my studio. And suddenly I see how the two have gotten out of balance. I have been *draining* myself instead of *using* myself.[12]

The image of myself as an empty shell comes to mind. I have not shed my skin as a snake does. I stand still waiting – waiting to be refilled. As I balance myself between art, teaching, store and child rearing I find it difficult to know what to let go. Is it because one capacity implicitly informs the other? How do I effectively use my energy, as opposed to letting it be drained and discarded?

Lindsay, 21 October 1999:

Have been actively writing again in my journal. I had stopped for several months. It had been hard to talk even to myself. To paraphrase a quote from Yeats – a writer (and artist) has to either focus on perfecting their life or perfecting their writing. It's impossible to do both.[13] I see the point but find it so discouraging. I want – need – to find ways to blend both into one continuous seam.

Lindsay, 21 November 1999:

I can feel myself at the edge of a pool of work to be made. I hesitate to immerse myself. Creating is a painful act. It requires absorption; withdrawing from my life enough to gain the perspective I need to distil it into visual form. Once I am in the pool and working I am OK. It is the initial jump that terrifies me.

Kay, 6 December 1999:

In response to your quote from Yeats that a writer (artist) has to focus on perfecting their writing or perfecting their life, I can't agree.

His view came from a particular context, influenced by culture as well as his gender. Across the channel and a bit later in the 1920s the artist Stella Bowen was living with the writer Ford Maddox Ford who, like Yeats, separated art from life and seemed to believe that the value of his writing would excuse his imperfect relationship to the women in his life. Unlike Ford, Bowen refused to separate life from art and said 'More than one thing matters'.[14] Drusilla Modjeska believes that Bowen's skill in conducting her personal relationships informed her practice. The perception and tact evident in her dealings with people contributed greatly to the quality of her portraits.

Perhaps if we can acknowledge the inter-relatedness of all aspects of life, including art, and recognise that at various times different parts take precedence, then we don't have to choose between art and life. It's more a matter of balance than choice.

Now balancing is hard. I don't think I ever get it right, but these days I seem to be able to take a longer view than I could when I was younger. I can allow life to take precedence at times without believing I've abandoned my practice. So perhaps (to continue your metaphor) it is possible to stitch the bits together in one continuous seam, and the odd, loose thread may not even be visible when you view the whole cloth!

Textile practice, like writing, offers such rich metaphorical possibilities for manifesting this idea that 'more than one thing matters'. The use of textile terms as a sign for connection are so deeply embedded in language that I'm making an ongoing collection of uses of the word 'tapestry' in this context, called of course 'The Rich Tapestry of Life'!

Lindsay, 7 January 2000:

Have you ever been so emotionally overwhelmed and physically overworked that when you actually see an end in sight you have a feeling of coming out from under a coma?

I am closing my retail business. The last day is 12 March 2000. From almost the beginning I have struggled to balance the heavy demands of retail business with the special needs of my daughter. My godmother died only 6 months after I took over the business. She named me as guardian of her two children. Sarah is autistic and to get her the special education she needed, I finally relinquished custody of her to the state of Missouri. Emilie moved in with me. Both girls were from orphanages in Romania. In effect I am Emilie's third mom.

The decision to close my business was difficult. I looked into every possibility to keep it open that would allow for less of my own involvement. The business is 30 years old – an institution in Chicago. I don't want to close it, but I also don't want to continue with it. I am worn out.

Writing these letters has been difficult. I am using them as a vehicle to analyse my current life and examine how my art is a direct extension of it. The process has at times been painful. I have been avoiding it this last month as I went through the decision to close my store.

Do you ever consider your art as therapeutic? I am often asked this question. There is no doubt that the repetitive gestures of weaving, knitting and stitching can be soothing. But I emphatically don't see my art itself as a therapeutic product. Because my work deals with illness, death and parenthood in a frank and blunt manner, it opens up a space for the viewer to make emotional connections. It is not unusual for me to receive letters from strangers who have seen my work and feel emotionally moved by it, as they have experienced an illness in the family or know of the difficulty of raising a child. My art opens up a dialogue within the viewer, posing questions they had perhaps not considered. I consider my work directly linked to all the textiles, sculptures and paintings, which record personal and national calamities – works of art that attempt to open our eyes so that change can occur.

Kay, 23 January 2000:

It's a Sunday morning, Tom is with his dad and the day stretches out before me, mine to do as I please.

I've been re-reading your unfinished letter of October 15.

Perhaps we're the first generation of women who expect to have it all, jobs, family and in our cases an art practice as well. I read a biography of Margaret Attwood, *the red shoes*, by Rosemary Sullivan[15] during the week between Christmas and the New Year. Attwood knew very early that she would be a writer. In the late fifties, such a choice seemed to put children out of the question. Thirty years on with a husband, two stepsons and a daughter, she noted that it was possible to manage writing and a family, but not a teaching job as well!

So no wonder you find the balance almost impossible to achieve. Sometimes being busy can be energising, but I've noticed that emotional difficulties just drain energy away so your image of yourself as an empty shell is understandable. I've found that ordering, repetitive activities have helped me to get through such times: weeding the garden, cleaning out the cupboards. The work was calming and if it didn't quite take your mind off the problem, there was the satisfaction of bringing order to a bit of your life, amid the emotional chaos.

I've been thinking about the symbolic connections we draw between cloth and skin. Perhaps that is why the rending of garments is part of the ritual of mourning in some cultures, relieving the unbearable pressure of the emotions, tearing cloth rather than cutting skin. Perhaps like the adolescent ritual of cutting ones own skin at times of unendurable tension, ripping cloth offers momentary relief from the pressure of uncontrollable changes.

I recently read the following lines in the poem *White Night* by Adrienne Rich.

> Light at a window. Someone up
> at this snail-still hour.
> We who work this way have often worked

in solitude. I've had to guess at her
sewing her skin together as I sew mine
though
with a different
stitch[16]

If we do construct our sense of self through language, perhaps that is why we use the word 'skin', for both the membrane that separates the body from the outside world, and as a metaphor for the psychic boundary of the self. Think of 'thin skinned', 'thick skinned'. Skin, a permeable membrane barely containing the forces of emotion.

It seems very apt to link writing to stitching, mind to body, in the construction of the self.[17] In adolescence the sense of self is so precarious, so easily unstitched. As you say, space to understand and make sense of the changes is essential. Perhaps all we can do as mothers is to provide that space, and perhaps be there to demonstrate the efficacy of mending rather than the quick relief of cutting it out.

You ask if I see my work as therapeutic.

I see my art and writing as a way of making sense of my experience, making sense of who I am, constructing my 'self' in fact. It is therapeutic in the sense that making and writing open up a space for reflection, enabling me to come to terms with loss and cope with the unpredictability of life.

I began this in the calm space of a Sunday but I'm finishing it in the hectic rush of a Tuesday.

Lindsay, 25 January 2000:

I had to laugh when I read of your habit to engage in repetitive activities when under emotional duress. How true! Emilie was in the hospital again last week. I became obsessed with cleaning. I couldn't relax until the house was fully scrubbed clean. I wanted to wipe out every last trace of Emilie's anger.

I keep asking myself, 'So now what?' A friend who is also closing her business commented that at least I know what I am doing with my life, taking care of Emilie. But I am not closing the store to take care of Emilie, I am already doing that. I am closing my store to take care of myself. People don't seem to understand just how important that, in and of itself, really is.

I enjoyed your comments on Margaret Attwood. I have been struggling against myself. My very core or being is as an artist. I speak clearest through a visual language. Wrapping around this core is Emilie, followed by family and friends. Then there are my academic interests followed by the need to earn money. Quilting the layers together takes sheer grit and determination. I need to get back to just three layers. Art, Emilie, family and friends. My money needs are greater now. Mortgage, child-rearing expenses, hospital bills, but I think I can do it. Time will tell won't it? If Margaret Attwood could do it, maybe I can too.

Lindsay, 14 February 2000:
    Emilie is in the hospital for the second time this year. I have to place her in a residential unit. She needs more therapeutic intervention than a day school and I alone can provide. The heartache is tremendous. I know in my bones that Em is going to be OK, but I hate having to send her away. She will be in the unit for a year or more. It is a decision based on love for her, but it feels like a failure on my part to provide for her.
    One thing I can say with certainty is that everyday I am grateful for my training in the visual arts. It trains one to be flexible, investigative and relentless in one's search for meaning. Without these skills, I don't think I could have carried Emilie as far as I have. Doctors, nurses, therapists and social workers are consistently surprised by the ingenuity I have used to reach out to her. They are now recommending some of my 'tricks' to other patients and their families.
    I wonder why art therapists depend so heavily on pen, paper and crayon to define emotions when the human need for touch is so well documented. Pen, paper and crayon are simply less tactile. These last few months I often found Emilie behind a chair in our living room weaving on a little tapestry loom, interlacing texture and colour. When the cloth became large enough, she would rub her fingers over the many textures again and again. Often when Em was on the edge of an anxiety attack, I would bring in bowls of rice or baskets of yarn for her to use to soothe herself. The stimulation of running her hands through uncooked rice or strands of mohair allowed her anxiety to mellow enough to the point where she could use words to define her feelings.

Kay, 12 March 2000:
    I liked your metaphor of the commitments in your life as a quilt stitched through with grit and determination. If the stitches are your days, taken individually they can be full of pain, the layers resisting your attempts to stitch them together, but seen as a continuum each day builds on the one before. Later, that part of the quilt (your life) with the pinpricks of blood,

the broken threads and missed stitches will be hardly noticeable in the context of the whole.

So don't give up!

One of my colleagues at the University of South Australia, Alison Mackinnon, wrote a book called *Love and Freedom*,[18] tracing the choices made by the first generation of women educated at universities in the U.K. and Australia during the early years of the twentieth century. Before contraception was safe and readily available, women who wanted careers had to choose between family and their vocation, which often meant between 'love and freedom' although some married but significantly didn't have children. Since the sixties, women have theoretically been able to have both, but at what cost!

At present I'm working on a huge community tapestry project interpreting the work of Australian writer and artist Barbara Hanrahan into woven tapestry.[19] As I sit weaving her images and words and discussing the process with viewers and the other weavers, I've become fascinated by the complexity of the idea of the 'mother' in our culture.

We're weaving one of Hanrahan's images called *Puppet-master*, which, despite the masculine form, she represents as a mother, a fierce, masked and frightening figure clutching a puppet child to her chest, twinned to a puppet head on her hand, with a row of grotesquely grinning puppet heads ranged along the top of the image like a Greek chorus.

It's an unsettling image of the power of the mother, of the tensions that pull between love and responsibility. Many visitors to the library, who admire the weaving, find the image too confronting. Barbara, who was born in 1939 and died in 1991, was of that generation of artists who chose a loving partnership but decided not to have children. All her energies were focused on her practice, which included both art and writing. Mothers and grandmothers proliferate as images in her work, the source of love and nurturing. Yet her images of women also expose the stifling conformity of feminine roles and reveal the inner tensions of women struggling to reconcile conflicting desires.

I was so moved by your description of the strategies you used to help Emilie to calm herself. They reminded me of Winnicott's notion of the 'transitional object', usually a textile that acts as a substitute for the mother as the child copes with the process of separation. Perhaps your bowls of rice and strands of mohair acted as transitional objects for Emilie? It is the tactile that is a significant quality of these objects, the softness, the silkiness, the warmth of a soft toy or piece of blanket, a metonymic substitute for the mother's body.

Tom has a new kitten. I'd forgotten how unbelievably soft fur can be and the pleasure of stroking her as she sits, purring, on my lap. Cuddling Mopsy (baby talk?) in his bed allows Tom to sink back into the tactile world of babyhood again while at the same time learning the pleasures of nurturing.

Perhaps for Emilie running strands of mohair through her hands, it is touch that will connect her to the world, repair the threads severed so early in her life, and mend the cloth that failed to hold her.

One of my friends returned from China last month with the gift of an indigo cloth for me. Exchanging these letters has reminded me of this practice of giving and receiving textiles. The cloth, a symbol of the reciprocity of relationships, the give and take of our growing friendship mapped through our letters.

Notes

1. C. Winnicott (ed.), *Home is Where We Start From: Essays by a Psychoanalyst,* U.S. edition (W.W. Norton & Co: New York, 1985).
2. Peggy Phelan, *Mourning Sex. Performing Public Memories,* p. 5.
3. Louise K.Kaplan, *Female Perversions,* p. 86.
4. Drusilla Modjeska, *Stravinsky's Lunch* (Pan Macmillan Australia: Sydney, 1999).
5. Stella Bowen's work can be seen in the U.K. at the National Portrait Gallery, London, and in Australia at the Art Gallery of South Australia, Adelaide, and the Australian War Memorial, Canberra. Cossington Smith's work can be seen in Australia at the National Gallery of Australia, Canberra, and in most eastern State and Regional Art Galleries as well as in the Holmes à Court Collection, Heytesbury, Western Australia.
6. D.W. Winnicott, *Playing and Reality, p.* 103. Modjeska used the term 'transitional space' for what Winnicott describes as 'potential space'. He says 'The potential space between baby and mother, between child and family, between individual and society or the world, depends on experience which leads to trust. It can be looked upon as sacred to the individual in that it is here that the individual experiences creative living'.
7. Virginia Woolf, *A Room of One's Own* (Penguin Modern Classics: Great Britain, 1965, first published 1928).
8. Jasleen Dhamija, 'The Ritual Uses of Textiles in India' a paper presented at the *Indian Textiles Seminar,* conducted by The Asian Arts Society of Australia at the Art Gallery of South Australia, 29 June 1996.
9. Rene Descartes, translated from Latin by Donald Cress, *Meditations on First Philosophy: In Which the Existence of God and the Distinction of the Soul from the Body are Demonstrated* (Hackett: Indianapolis, in 1979, first published in 1641).
10. Winifred Gallagher, *Working on God,* pp. 129–130.
11. Thich Nhat Hanh, Arnold Kotler (ed.), *Peace is Every Step: The Path of Mindfulness in Everyday Life* (Bantam Books: New York, 1991).
12. Anne Truitt, *Prospect: The Journey of an Artist,* p. 95.
13. Alexandra Johnson, *The Hidden Writer: Diaries and the Creative Life* (Anchor: New York, 1997), p. 13.
14. Stella Bowen, *Drawn from Life, A Memoir,* p. 271.

15. Rosemary Sullivan, *the red shoes: Margaret Attwood Starting Out* (Harper Flamingo: Canada, 1998).
16. Adrienne Rich, 'White Night' in *The Fact of a Doorframe: Poems Selected and New 1950–1982, p.* 207.
17. I am grateful to Gail Jones for this insight in her essay 'Softness: Four Meditations on the Poetics of Cloth' in the catalogue *From within, Jane Whitely, Works in Cloth, pp.* 7–8.
18. Alison Mackinnon, *Love and Freedom* (Cambridge University Press, U.K. 1997).
19. *Barbara Hanrahan Community Tapestry Project*; a series of woven tapestries based on the work of Hanrahan, woven by community weavers in the State Library of South Australia, Adelaide and Thebarton Branch Library, City of West Torrens for the Hawke Centre, University of South Australia. The project was coordinated by Kay Lawrence assisted by Kirsty Darlaston and Karen Russell during 1999 and 2000.

Bibliography

Bowen, Stella, *Drawn from Life, A Memoir* (Sydney: Picador, 1999).

Gallagher, Winifred, *Working on God* (Random House: New York, 1999).

Johnson, Alexandra, *The Hidden Writer: Diaries and the Creative Life, (New York:* Anchor, 1997).

Kaplan, J. Louise, *Female Perversions* (London: Penguin Books 1991).

Mackinnon, Alison, *Love and Freedom* (Cambridge: Cambridge University Press, U.K. 1997).

Modejska, Druisilla, *Stravinsky's Lunch* (Sydney, Australia: Pan Macmillan, 1999).

Phelan, Peggy, *Mourning Sex. Performing Public Memories* (USA: Routledge, 1997).

Rich, Adrienne, *The Fact of a Doorframe. Poems Selected and New 1950–1982* (New York London: W.W. Norton and Co, 1984).

Truitt, Anne, *Prospect: The Journey of an Artist* (New York: Putnam, 1996)

Truitt, Anne, *Day: The Journey of an Artist* (New York: Patheon, 1982).

Truitt, Anne, *Turn: The Journey of an Artist* (New York: Thames and Hudson, 1979).

Winnicott, D.W., *Playing and Reality* (London: Tavistock, 1971).

Woolf, Virginia, *A Room of One's Own* (London: Penguin, 1928).

MIGRANT TEXTILES: BURDENS, BUNDLES AND BAGGAGE

Barbara Layne

'Collecting is an essential human feature that originates in the need to tell stories, but for which there are neither words nor other conventional modes. Hence, collecting is a story, and everyone needs to tell it.'

Mieke Bal[1]

A passport filled with immigration stamps of the plumed quetzal, a symbol of Guatemala's nationalism, marks a series of annual trips made between 1983 and 1997. The purpose was to collect Maya textiles and enjoy the perfect highland sun on the shores of shimmering volcanic lakes. Over the years this passion swelled to more than 300 collected pieces of stunning designs and innovative techniques, the evidence of a visual language passed down through generations of weavers. Through experiences with Maya weavers I developed an ever-increasing greater awareness of the importance cloth can play in the social negotiations of a culture. From the everyday garment to the ceremonial cloth of the *cofradía* (a religious social order), textiles embody complex and dynamic relationships of power, gender and identity. This understanding was to become the basis for my current studio practice, one which recognises the value and relevance of traditional textile work within a world racing toward a digitally enhanced future.

'Ownership is the most intimate relationship that one can have to objects. Not that they come alive in him; it is he who lives in them.'

Walter Benjamin[2]

After moving from the United States to Quebec in 1989, I began to critically examine the transference of cultural property, considering the cross-border movement of my personal belongings and the further displacement of the collection of Maya textiles to northern lands. This resulted in the 1992 installation, *Boundary Problems*, which incorporated beeswax replicas of objects from my textile collection.

By inserting the wax copies into a floor map of Montreal's Dorval airport, I was able to consider not only the shifting of objects, but my own nomadic experience.

> 'Reproduced in wax, they exist in a transitory state, inexact replicas, never to be cast. I consider my own (relocated) position in Montreal – too assimilated to claim immigrant status – too different to feel at home.'[3]

In the following year the installation *Destinations* was developed for the Contemporary Gallery of the Museum for Textiles in Toronto. This project involved the study and duplication of objects from the museum's archives. Again, wax replicas were created, using a global sampling of the collection. Beeswax replaced the original material evidence of place, rendering all forms with a fragrant, golden glow. These new standardised objects were inserted into a room-sized map of Toronto's Pearson International Airport,

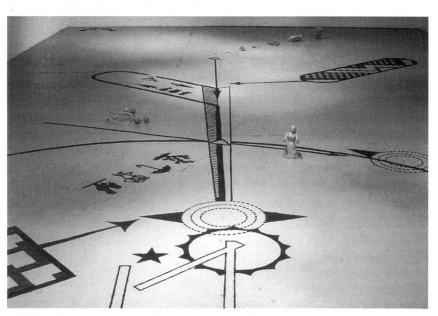

Barbara Layne: **Boundary Problems** (1992), detail
mixed media installation

a technological and cultural crossroads. The intersecting straight lines that are the runways define points of arrival and departure. By portraying them with strips of fabric hand-stitched into the gallery's industrial carpet, the diagram becomes imprecise and unpredictable, recalling human situations that accompany passage through borderlands.

Continuing to reference textiles and collections, two distinctly different projects followed: *Electronic Textiles: Hacking the Museum* (1996) and *Maya Textiles: Visions of Identity* (a collaborative project with Karen Michelsen, 1997). Both projects used the juxtaposition of objects, texts and images to address issues of migration and its relationship to textiles. These installations created flexible spaces, open to variable interpretations. The construction of multi-encoded environments can more closely echo the complex circumstances in which textiles function.

Maya Textiles: Visions of Identity

Thirty years of civil war in Guatemala began as a systematic repression of the indigenous people by the military dictatorship in the mid-1960s. Approximately two hundred thousand Maya people were killed or disappeared[4] and countless more tortured and displaced. Although weaving continued, production lessened as energy was diverted toward the business of survival. As a traveller through the highlands of Guatemala it was difficult to learn about the conflict since media reports conformed to official governmental versions. The usually friendly Maya knew that candid conversations could be dangerous as infiltrators were not uncommon amidst indigenous people. My exchanges with weavers were often limited to discussions of textile materials and techniques, or girl-chat about the latest North American fashion trends.

I learned to speak Spanish from women who work on backstrap looms (see colour plate 3). I learned that it was not unusual to use the word *lana* for acrylic as well as its direct translation, wool; and *seda* (silk) could equally be applied to rayon yarns. On the other hand, cotton thread, *algodon,* has a highly specialised series of names, relating to colour or lustre or number of ply or place of origin. *Jasepe* yarns are tie-dyed to a pattern before weaving. The precious *ixcaco* is an indigenous brown cotton that is hand spun and woven into ceremonial or other special fabrics. Then there's *aleman,* a fine and luxurious red from Germany, and *brillo, sedalina, madeja,* etc …

The specificity of cotton nomenclature is but one example of the relationship between a material language and identity. These twisted bits of cellulose fibre signify a unique system of value. Whereas acrylic and silk are imported, and sheep were introduced during colonial times, cotton is indigenous to Central America, and although the affirmation of Maya identity is considered a recent phenomenon,[5] the level of discernment of cotton threads demonstrates a longstanding appreciation for the indigenous.

Such detail in the language of textiles becomes even more complex when compounded by unique approaches to spinning, dyeing, plying, plaiting, stitching, and weaving and through the usage of *traje*.[6]

Travelling Light

Limiting personal luggage to what can fit into a small, book-size backpack lends an illusion of invisibility and allows me to slide discreetly into the cracks of the overcrowded travel vans and ancient Blue Bird school buses rescued from mothball fleets. However, I am not completely unnoticed, as the netted bundle of live crabs at my feet wave their menacing claws and the child standing on the seat behind me smashes her lunch of gooey yams into my hair.

Burdens

I was introduced to Catarina Cuc Tzep on my first trip to Guatemala in 1983 and we have maintained a friendship ever since. She wears the traditional *traje* of her village of Nahualá, an indigo *corte* (skirt) with a colourfully embroidered *randa* embellishing the seam, her *huipil* brocaded with linear patterning of plants and animals. She rides the predawn bus with an enormous bundle of cloth, heading for the tourist markets in the streets of Antigua, Panajachel or Chichicastenango. At the top of her stack of cloth are *typicos*, the coarsely woven, inexpensive tourist textiles. She also carries a few pieces she hopes to sell on behalf of other weavers in her village.

For the few buyers who demonstrate an appreciation for *traje*, Catarina will dig deeper in the pile to find the more 'authentic' treasures, such as the stained clothing her children have outgrown, or the fine weavings she has made on indigo warps, filled with silken images of deer and trees and quetzals. When necessary, she will sell *un antiguo*, a rare piece from a deceased family member. Walking through the streets alone, she balances the cloth bundle squarely on top of her head, a young child perpetually slung onto her back.

'Cultural baggage', from an ethnographic perspective, is not a nuisance, but an opening. It can be a corrective for the unacknowledged and unexamined stereotypes that 'humans' bring to cultural encounters. It can even be more.'

Barbara Kirschenblatt-Gimblett[7]

Dissipation

I purchase a large sisal bag for the growing collection of cloths acquired from dozens of weavers. Textiles that have been impregnated with the mixed odours of wood fires, baby piss and the sweet smelling sweat of bodies made from corn. Thrown precariously on top of the buses, the bags seem to defy the law of gravity, always arriving intact at the next town. But were these the same cloths that had been hoisted above? The open structure of the net holds the layers of cloth, while the mountain winds begin to dissipate the scents and the debris. A final washing after arriving home removes other traces.

Classification

Karen Michelsen, a Peruvian-born textile artist and researcher, offered to catalogue my collection. We sorted through the piles of brilliantly coloured cloths, matching them to the odd notes scribbled on paper. The textiles were categorised according to the village of origin, exotic combinations of Spanish saints and indigenous names such as *San Lucas Tolimán, Santiago Atitlán* and *Todos Santos Cuchumatán*. I relayed stories surrounding the acquisition of the collection while Karen researched systems of classification and carefully articulated the provenance for each cloth. A database was compiled and the requisite label was sewn into each piece.

But the textiles longed to be understood in more complex terms.

'You consider, count, review the collection. Then the relationships that have broken down your careful categories. You toss aside tools, are comforted by the long continuous thread of running water that rattles into a pail.'

Verona[8]

Karen suggested a project which would challenge the limitations of the system we had just established, one that would display the textiles without a descriptive (prescriptive) label. The resulting exhibition, *Maya Textiles: Visions of Identity*, was held at the Marsil Museum in St. Lambert, Quebec in 1997. Eleven 'visual essays' were developed, displaying not only cloth but providing a context that addressed the complex political and cultural situation in Guatemala. The restraints of classification were abandoned as the beauty of the cloth was contrasted with the social realities and human struggle of the Maya.

> 'It is left up to him to interpret things the way he understands them, and thus the narrative achieves an amplitude that information lacks.'
>
> Walter Benjamin[9]

The images were culled from a variety of sources, including a fashion magazine, tourist postcard, and published and unpublished photographs. Within each of the large black and white photographs, a single textile was highlighted with a silk-screened transparent colour. A corresponding cloth from the collection was displayed alongside the image and accompanied by a quote addressing a particular social situation (For example, a text from Rigoberta Menchú: 'What hurts Indians most is that our costumes are considered beautiful, but it's as if the person wearing it didn't exist.[10]) The 'visual essays' brought together disparate fragments, intertwining multiple stories of Maya endurance, struggle and hope. Information was not presented in didactic terms but within a flexible, narrative space. The installation was a site of transformation, a new location in which to encourage thoughtfulness about the relationship of cloth and human experience.

Electronic Textiles: Hacking the Museum

Systems of classification as normally seen in museum collections raise questions of cultural identity, power and ownership. The exhibition project *Electronic Textiles: Hacking the Museum* attempted to interfere with the authority of the museum by disrupting the system of indexation. The project involved the transmission of images of textiles from the Marsil Museum in Quebec to the Glassbox Gallery in England via the Internet.[11] In the exhibition space, digital images were received and 'reconstituted' into material forms through stitching on fabric. Each day as I was preparing images at the museum's storage area in Montreal, the gallery in Britain was filled with the activity of embroidery, couching, beading and machine stitching.

> 'The computer has developed into a versatile tool for modeling systems that reflect our ideas about how the world is organised....

Part of the early work in any medium is the exploration of the
border between the representational world and the actual world.'
Janet H. Murray[12]

The aim of *Electronic Textiles: Hacking the Museum* was to reopen the
potential of the collected object using a digital interface. In this regard I was
more that ably assisted by Janet Bezzant of Manchester Metropolitan
University. She facilitated the Salford links. The computer and the
communication possibilities offered by the Internet can establish active
spaces and provide a fluid architecture in which to explore alternative
positions. The capacity to gather, store, manipulate and transmit
information can extend ways in which the world can be perceived.

Digital Cargo

Taken from the highly regulated temperature and humidity controlled
environment of the museum, the images are packaged and launched into
Cyberspace. As digital files, these textiles enter a matrix of interwoven
data, the Internet, through a method called packet switching. When a file
is transferred from one place to another, the Transmission Control Protocol
(TCP) divides the file into smaller portions, encoding each one with the
destination address.

The data packets may take different routes commingling with foreign
segments of information. Upon arrival to the destination they are
reassembled into the original file. Central to the *Electronic Textiles* project
is the notion of transformation or transition as the Net narrows the distance
between Montreal and Manchester, linking the Marsil Museum and the
Glass Box Gallery.

The opportunity to explore the storage areas of a museum is a glorious
adventure. But before entering any museum's archives, the card catalogue is
mandatorily researched. The system of classification at the Marsil Museum
is delineated by function and gender, distinguishes between adult's and
children's wear, and has a small section of non-Western dress. While this
might be useful for ordering the collection, such systems reinforce stereotypical
hierarchies and establish fixed definitions that are not realistic or reflective
of the changing world. Taxonomic processes limit the understanding of cultural
objects as well as the communities in which they have been created. Removing
an object from its original context and reframing it within the museum's
encoded system creates new meaning. Helen Coxall argues that women's
lives, in particular, have been rendered invisible by institutional collection

policies. A woman's possessions are often relegated to the category of the domestic, unvalued and erased from the realm of acknowledged history.[13]

> 'Although women from across class boundaries made and designed things throughout their lives, this particular activity remains on the margins. This is compounded by the fact that the 'things' are clothes and they were made locally, mostly at home ... 'home' was a more fragmented place than the frozen space of patriarchal mythology.'
>
> Cheryl Buckley[14]

During several visits to the storage area of the Marsil Museum, Cynthia Cooper, Curator of Costume, assisted in the navigation through the stacks, locating the items I had noted from the card catalogue. The selected textiles were photographed directly into a laptop computer with a low resolution QuickCam camera.

Each image underwent a 'normalisation' process through manipulation in Photoshop, rendering them similar in size and surface treatment. In Photoshop all extraneous background 'noise' was eliminated and then the photo passed through a variety of dithers and filters. These stylisations reduced the memory size of the image, yet also exaggerated arbitrary characteristics that had not previously been considered: a subtle shadow, a topstitch detail. The catalogue system was disregarded and, in many cases, references to gender, function and age were blurred along with material identification and point of origin. In this process of declassification, a mourning veil, a gentleman's top hat and a well-worn nurse's cap receive equal treatment, bearing only cursory resemblance to the original object.

Through this process of digitising, the textiles were radically altered. It was not merely a material presence or physical appearance that was affected but an essence even essential to the very nature of an object. In 'The Work of Art in an Age of Mechanical Reproduction' Walter Benjamin proposes that the original authentic object possesses an *aura* and warns us of its loss through reproduction.[15] It might seem that through these digital manipulations the essence of the textile was lost. However, I contend that an object appropriated by the museum has already suffered loss of authenticity through the process of relocation.

Gloves 1987–16–01
  Pale blue synthetic knit mittens. Long. Pattern created through opening in knit. 1950s.

Furthermore, the classification system is a transformative process, turning artefacts into simulations. Since I was not permitted to directly access the material objects in storage, my initial selections and assumptions were made by studying the text-based card catalogue.

Chain Purse 1986–03–05
Engraved at the top, 'Presented to Miss Bradshaw by her sincere friends on her leaving Carrier Pet. 1910' (She was a village nurse all her life).

By the time I physically encountered the material objects, meaning had already been established based on information cited in the index cards. Consider Jean Baudrillard's assertion that material does not equal real. Simulations precede and engender a 'hyperreality' in which origins are forgotten and that the 'real is no longer real'.[16] With *Electronic Textiles: Hacking the Museum*, I proposed to release the hyperreal object from the containment of the storage space and from the closed circuit of simulacra, encouraging a revitalisation of the textile object through human activity.

The Glass Box Gallery exists as a vulnerable, exposed space of glass walls, white tile floor and gigantic skylight. An observation deck provides a voyeuristic view into the site. Situated inside the space was a computer

Barbara Layne: **Electronic Textiles: Hacking the Museum** (1997), detail installation

terminal and four large glass tables serving as work stations. Each was etched with text from the Marsil's card catalogue corresponding to the image being constructed at that work station.

Fox Stole 1990–24
   Brown fox stole, made of two entire foxes. Label: J.V. Quinn, Furrier, Montreal, Canada. Donor says these furs belonged to her mother.

The pristine gallery evoked a scientific laboratory or a workshop for textile conservation and research. Each worker / stitcher (students from the University of Salford's Visual Culture and Arts course)[17] donned a white lab coat with the image of their labour imprinted on the backs of the coat, locating them in the space with a sense of authority. Involved in the various acts of couching, chain stitch embroidery, beading and machine stitching, the workers became the primary actors in an attempt to 'perform' the museum.

Man's Coat 1985–83
   Coat of black wool. Double breasted knee length. 1898. Worn by Honorius Richer (1874–1952) of St. Andre Avellin at the age of 24 for his wedding with Malvina Jackson-Boyer (was adopted which explains why she has two last names) in 1898.

During the first week of the installation I was transmitting images and exchanging e-mail with the stitchers (whom I had not yet met). We discussed the working procedures and the sewing technique to be used for each image. Initially, they were uncomfortable and somewhat embarrassed to be sewing in the space they referred to as 'the fishbowl'. Visitors to the gallery were able to watch from outside the space or enter it to inquire about such peculiar activity (sewing!) taking place in such a public venue. The stitchers received a number of derogatory remarks from inadvertent passers-by, such as 'Hey babe, can you repair my pants?'
   In the e-mail exchanges of the first days, we discussed the unpredictable nature of tableau vivant and noted other installations in which textile work was produced in the gallery. Activities such as the seated knitter in Anne Hamilton's *A Round* (1993) or Regina Frank's *Herme's Mistress* (1994–5) in which the artist actively 'beads' her e-mail messages around the circumference of the flared hem of her dress, affirming the importance of needlework in the dynamic history of women. Through the process of hand stitching, the *Electronic Textiles* workers began to feel more located in the space and came to appreciate the significance of their public performance.

rem acu tetigisti
(A Latin phrase, literally 'you've touched the thing with a needle', meaning that the point is fully grasped).[18]

Their embarrassment soon turned to a creative anger, and eventually resulted in an installation of their own collaboration in a nearby site. Their exhibit appropriated elements from the Glass Box installation (lab coats, stitching, etc.) and a poetic text on the celebration of embroidery interwoven with the inane comments they had scavenged from the *Electronic Textiles* experience.

Border Crossing

Having completed the digital transmissions, I prepared for departure to England for my first viewing of the exhibition. A fierce snowstorm invaded Manchester and the residence at the old train station at Heaton Chapel lacks central heating. I carefully fold and pack wool sweaters, thermal boots, a heavy coat, long johns and the black dress for the vernissage. Carry-on luggage includes the laptop computer, a stack of slides and the words borrowed from theorists and philosophers to support my presentation at the ETN (European Textile Network) Conference. The baggage is heavy.

Over the past several decades, cultural theorists, museum specialists and artists have contributed to the ongoing critique of the museum. Definitive writings by Edward Said, Stuart Hall, James Clifford, Susan Pearce, Susan Stewart and works of art such as Fred Wilson's provocative *Mining the Museum*[19] have examined issues related to diaspora and the relocation of cultural objects. Wilson's poignant juxtaposition of slave shackles displayed alongside silver vessels demonstrates a rethinking not only of the hierarchy of objects but of power relationships and conditions of ownership. One elegant, one horrific, the placement of these disparate pieces of metalwork is not typical of museum display, however their interlinked relationship to one another is undeniable.

Museums will continue to be highly problematic and we will still be magnetically drawn to them. Who is not transfixed by the sight of the Temple of Dendur, the fifteenth century BC temple and gate from Egypt, relocated stone-by-stone to the Metropolitan Museum of Art? And I can still recall the excitement of holding down the painfully stiff button on the glass case at the Brooklyn Museum of Art that provides the dim lighting for viewing the barely visible and utterly miraculous needle-knitted Paracas Textile.

In spite of fictitious constructions and biased systems of classification, museums provide access to treasures that can stimulate the imagination, fill the eyes with beauty and wonder, enticing us with myth and awe.

Museums have been reconsidering their roles in response to the changing socio-cultural climate. While the collection is still central to the institution, most museums are increasing their public programming to include more educational activities, workshops, informative web sites and other interactive projects. In some exceptional cases, museums have made remarkable progress in returning ethnographic objects to cultural groups that have rightfully reclaimed ownership. Other institutions are brave enough to sponsor innovative artists' interventions such as projects by Fred Wilson or James Luna.

However, the museum visitor should remain cautious and conscientious, keeping in mind the historical context of the museum. Textiles present a particular set of problems, as museums have a tendency to consider them historic relics rather than part of an ongoing tradition of innovation. Usually associated with women's work, textiles can represent resistance and endurance in which the acts of making, selling and wearing become political acts. Embedded in the patterns, colours, structures and textures of cloth are the personal expression of an individual and the legacy of a culture. From the celebrated ritual fabric to the everyday utility wrap, these highly encoded cloths may also become the desired, exoticised and collected property of the privileged. In the move from private to public, these textiles are not only physically displaced; they also become signs representing the act of relocation.

Maya Textiles: Visions of Identity and *Electronic Textiles: Hacking the Museum* provided an opportunity to reconsider collection policies and to engage the museum through alternative display practices. Textiles were taken from the stasis of forgotten storage compartments and thrust into new narratives, re-released into a context of living traditions. These altered textiles enter negotiable spaces of transition where cultures meet and hybrids are formed. The combining of exhibition spaces and electronic interventions create alternative possibilities for museum display as new technologies extend the limitations of physical boundaries and systems of classification. This reframing results in an invigoration of the textile object into a new pattern of discovery, translating space into place, gesture into identity. Through the physical and virtual shifting of a textile object we can acknowledge the accomplishments of women.

Like many achievements in textile, these projects involved extended networks of people, including curators, co-ordinators, technical specialists and volunteers. In keeping with the tradition of textile labour, nearly all involved were women. The *Maya Textiles: Visions of Identity* project required a dynamic group of people involved in the Maya struggle. We were fortunate to have the assistance of various human rights support groups and individuals. Feedback was provided by a group of recently exiled Mayas who had relocated to Ontario only weeks before. The project also received encouragement from the controversial Rigoberta Menchú, who received the Nobel Peace Prize in 1992 for her testimony of the Maya struggle in Guatemala. Similarly, *Electronic Textiles: Hacking the Museum* also created an international network of volunteers and supporters. In 1996, only a small percentage of Internet users were women and the project was the impetus for many of the participants to engage in their first e-mail experience. My initial introduction to the sewing volunteers was through electronic means, and other activities, such as an interview for the journal *Act*, was conducted partially online.[20] The Internet facilitated communication and helped shape the new community involved with the project.

These projects also provide a platform from which to question my own relationship to privilege and ownership. What does it mean to possess the material production of another culture? What is the function of a personal collection and how can it be best used? What responsibilities come with ownership? I am fortunate to have access to this rich resource that can illustrate various techniques and design elements, a learning and teaching collection that can promote discussions about the displacement of cloth and the migration of people.[21]

Textiles are not the cargo that is transported in our personal baggage, but a vehicle in which to become more fully engaged in the experience of being. We can become mesmerised in the folds, hold conversations in the web, and find complications in the texture. They tell the stories of a vintage Dior in a pile of unsorted thrift-store clothing, of being rooted in a wool plaid, flirting along the bouncy hem of a flared skirt, or admiring the brilliant red *algodon* that is the resilience of the Maya.

Notes

1. Mieke Bal, 'Telling Objects: A Narrative Perspective on Collecting' in John Elsner and Roger Cardinal (eds), *The Cultures of Collecting*, p. 103.
2. Walter Benjamin, 'Unpacking My Library', in Hannah Arendt (ed.) *Illuminations*, p. 67.
3. From artist's statement for Boundary Problems.
4. The term 'disappearance' was first coined in Guatemala.
5. See Carol Hendrickson, *Weaving Identities: Construction of Dress and Self in a Highland Guatemala Town*, Texas: University Of Texas Press, 1995, back cover, and Soel Rodas

Calderon's essay for the exhibition, *Maya Textiles: Visions of Identity* at http://alcor.concordia.ca/~textiles

6.   *Traje* includes all traditional clothing and accoutrements of Maya dress.

7.   Barbara Kirschenblatt-Gimblett, 'Confusing Pleasures', in Barbara Kirschenblatt-Gimblett (ed.), *Destination Culture*, p. 214.

8.   From an unpublished essay by Verona (D.L. Pughe).

9.   Walter Benjamin, 'The Storyteller', in Hannah Arendt (ed.), *Illuminations*, p. 89.

10.   Rigoberta Menchú, *I, Rigoberta Menchú*, Elisabeth Burrgos-Debray (ed.), 1984, p. 204.

11.   Janet Bezzant graciously coordinated this project, in conjunction with the 5th Annual European Textile Network Conference in March 1996.

12.   Janet H. Murray, *Hamlet on the Holodeck: The Future of Narrative in Cyberspace*, p. 92.

13.   Helen Coxall, 'Re-presenting Marginalized Groups in Museums: The computer's 'second nature'?' in The Cutting Edge, Women's Research Group (eds.) *Desire by Design: Bodies, Territories and New Technologies*, pp. 123–138.

14.   Cheryl Buckley, 'On the Margins: Theorizing the History and Significance of Making and Designing Clothes at Home', in Barbara Burman (ed.), *The Culture of Sewing: Gender, Consumption and Home Dressmaking*, p. 57.

15.   Walter Benjamin, 'The Work of Art in the Age of Mechanical Reproduction', in Hannah Arendt (ed.) *Illuminations*, pp. 217–252.

16.   Jean Baudrillard, 'The Precession of Simulacra', in Brian Wallace (ed.), *Art After Modernism*, pp. 253–282.

17.   With thanks to the course leader, Karen Borland, for her commitment to the project. The production team included Julie Clark, Jean Gaunt, Mavis Hardman, Denise Hayes, Alex Herbert, Joanne Pollack and computer technician Nicola Teece.

18.   Eugene Ehrlich, *Amo, Amas, Amat and More*, p. 247.

19.   See Lisa G. Corrin, *Mining the Museum*, 1994.

20.   'Hacking the Museum: Electronic Textiles', an online interview and discussion between Janis Jefferies and Barbara Layne, in John Gange (ed.), *ACT 4: Art Technology, Technique*, pp. 138–146.

21.   I taught at the University of South Carolina, Columbia, SC from 1982 to 1989 and at Concordia University in Montreal, Quebec from 1989 to the present.

RE-CONSTRUCTING CHINESE

Greg Kwok Keung Leong

Traditional notions of identity have been based around paradigms of a centre. In more recent times, concepts of de-centred identity have developed. These diametrically opposed visions have given rise to the struggle to define a personal sense of 'cultural identity' so often expressed in the literary, film, visual and performing art work of Asian Australian artists. This paper focuses on my recent body of work, *Remembering Chinese*[1], a collection of deceptively Chinese garments and accessories, and is an examination of the tension between the cultural identities we construct for ourselves – and, as visual artists, express through our practice – and others construct for us. More importantly it is an attempt to connect to, and, in some measure, reconcile, the two cultures my mother was born into – Chinese and Australian. In re-constructing her history as an (at times) uncomfortable journey through hostile cultures, I have used the meanings of costume as both symbolic and subversive devices.

Chinese costume, as Claire Roberts puts it,

> '... has long been a way to identify people's position within the social hierarchy. The Chinese character *fu* means clothing or dress. But that same Chinese character has a wide range of other connotations, including to serve, to obey, and even to be in mourning. There exists the closest relationship between clothing and ritual, in today's language, social standing, functions and duties. As these connotations and meanings suggest, the individual and the body are subjugated to particular social needs.'[2]

My use of costume as the principal conceit for both a public confessional process and a private act of cultural reclamation is more than an acknowledgement of the power of dress to express the 'social life and ... the cultural history of place ... the beliefs, aspirations and the self-expressions of the individual and society.'[3] Although there is very much a reference to the meaning of traditional dress, and a reverence for its psychological power, it is also an appropriative strategy to locate a centre that one has long ago wandered from. The work exploits the viewer's immediate associative connection between the exotic and the seductive, while surprising, when, on closer investigation, the garments yield many other secrets, many of which have little to do with the 'traditional' (dis)guise they have come dressed in.

This surprise is generally unanticipated because the garments are of a generic 'ancient' Chinese style, designed to inveigle and seduce at first glance, and are carefully installed to affect a historical display. But Joanne Entwistle and Elizabeth Wilson remind us that

> '... dress in everyday life cannot be separated from the living, breathing, moving body it covers. The importance of the body to dress is such that encounters with dress divorced from the body are strangely alienating. This can sometimes be strongly felt in the museum costume display ... such displays remind us that they are, after all art / craft objects in their own right as well as being constituent parts of the dress / body performance that constitutes identity.... In *Le Plaisir du Texte*, Roland Barthes suggests that *jouissance* ... arises at the point of the gap, and, while he is primarily discussing literature, he uses the example of the gap between waistband and jumper that reveals a glimpse of bare skin. The exhibit of garments unworn suggests a different yet equally momentous and even mysterious gap; for by their very lifelessness, the gowns remind us of the life that they were destined to adorn.'[4]

The superficially sensuous nature of the garments in *Remembering Chinese* – with their gorgeous colour and their sumptuous materials – suggest another reality under the surface, or indeed a *sur*reality, that museum pieces do not normally possess. The details of personal narrative and national political debate, screen printed on the fabric surface, disallows the viewer from merely revelling in the sensuality of cloth. Once read, these texts become sites of subversive argument.

I am therefore particularly attracted to the idea that clothing, while making declarations of identity, and evoking flesh and blood to hang from, can also work in subversive ways. The garments in *Remembering Chinese* are glamorous and extravagant in the way that costumes for the Sydney Gay and Lesbian Mardi Gras are. In an analysis of how costume operates in this famous event, Glynis Jones observes:

'Mardi Gras highlights the importance of clothing as a powerful and sophisticated communication system and what has been expressed here is a complex mix of personal subcultural and community issues ... clothing ... is primarily an attempt – either consciously or on a more subtle level – to conform to some ideal, whether that be mainstream or sub cultural.'

and,

'In addition to using costume to subvert the norms of the wider community, it is also used by subcultures as a way of actively claiming their identity within their own community. The clothing worn by many participants in the Mardi Gras parade is their *sub*cultural dress.'[5]

Coming from two minority cultures within Australia – Asian and gay – I have found costume a perfect vehicle for the declaration of dual cultural identity.

'Cultural identity' is clearly not defined by selecting the dominant culture (white, Anglo-Saxon) from among a plethora of cultures in a multicultural society, nor, going to the other extreme, framed as a sanitised construct of inter-racial relations. What are the pitfalls of following the various models and approaches to an investigation of cultural identity? Nikos Papastergiadis signals in his preface to a collection of dialogues on diaspora that he intends to 'contest the conventional models, which either reduced cultural identity to an exotic commodity, or coded it within an 'us' and 'them' hierarchy.' And he further adds, that 'in an age of globalised cultural dissemination and the return of vicious ethno-chauvinists, we need to propose new visions of identity that go beyond the dangerous calls for purity and the outdated claims of universalism.'[6]

Both these approaches – of defining culture either through exclusivity or some idealistic blanket globalism – ironically, essentially marginalise racial/cultural groups. Such approaches would disallow the possibility of the many distinctive differences between the different types of Chinese Australians that clearly exist in Australia today.[7]

In my case, while I am a relatively recent migrant (1981, when I was 35 years old), my mother is third generation Australian-born Chinese. My understanding of Australian culture has been deeply coloured by my mother's unhappy account of it.

My mother's father was a late example of the Chinese migrant who came to Australia to run a business. He had the general store in Blackheath in New South Wales. He married a locally born half Chinese Australian woman whose only real knowledge of her own mother was her European name on the birth certificate. My great-grandmother had apparently been cast out by the Chinese family she had become involved with through marriage. This reverse racism underscores, in somewhat horrific terms, the inability of the early Chinese migrants to assimilate – the marriage of a Chinese man to a European must have been a matter of humiliation for the family, and totally unacceptable.

My grandfather was, on the other hand, denied permanent residence – this was in the first two decades of this century.[8] My mother and her three siblings were born in Australia. She was born in 1918. Not only were the first Chinese settlers despised by white Australians, they kept to themselves, and my mother's family would have been no different. Although born Australian, my mother had no chance, with the fiercely anti-Asian ethos of the time, of successfully being assimilated into a western culture. My nieces, on the other hand, all born after 1970, have reaped the benefits of a positive multicultural environment. They have grown up *Australian*, in the best sense – feeling neither outcast nor the need to hang on to their parents' original culture at the expense of the one they were born into. They have not had to suffer the heartache of uprooting from one's home – without having had the choice of refusing – and re-locating in unwelcoming climes.

Diaspora, for many immigrant artists, is necessarily a site of hybridity, because there is a constant dialogue between what we might consider the original 'homeland' and the adopted homeland. A further complication is the fact that for many thousands of immigrant Chinese, the diasporic experience is two-tiered. The 'original' homeland is only a myth of which we have no first-hand experience. The Chinese of Hong Kong, Malaysia, Singapore, Vietnam, Taiwan and so on, who have never lived in China, can have no 'genuine' understanding of an aboriginal Chineseness. Or is this merely an illusory ideal, demanded by our need to focus on a centre, and which we have been (mis)led to believe would cure us of our diasporic malaise?

Part of the strategy in my examination of these issues is the referencing of the Chinese language and its position in my personal cultural history.[9]

It can be argued that the universal cultural focal point for the Chinese is their language. No matter where the Chinese person is from, no matter what their dialect or country of adoption is, the one constant is the written language. Referencing a language – the most important system of signs identifying the uniqueness of any culture – is crucial to cultural reclamation.

And yet if one is arguing the case for a concept of de-centred identity, is the use of a centring device – for language is one – appropriate? The Chinese language, however, is only universal in its *written* form. Depending on the dialect a Chinese person speaks, he may or may not be understood by another Chinese. Just as the English and Celtic languages are totally different, spoken Chinese dialects are equally mutually foreign. Chinese accents are give-aways to the speaker's origins, and often used against him or her as a sign of alienness, because of difference.

In addition, if a Chinese person was born and brought up in a country other than China, usage and accent are absolute markers. The Cantonese in Hong Kong, the Hakka in Singapore, the Vietnamese Chinese and so on are all marked by their Chinese (and for that matter – although it is not generally obvious to European Australians – their English) accents.

The Chinese language therefore can be considered both a centring and de-centring device when referenced in my work, and *Remembering* is therefore not a simple act of recalling a mother tongue, long neglected and forgotten through lack of use and through abandoning the study of it at the age of ten in Hong Kong. My mother had thought it would be more useful for me to learn French as my second language at the English language school I attended.

The semiotic richness of Chinese lies in the specific multi-layered nature of the language. While it is not possible to expand on that here, it is important to note that Chinese text has always been integral to Chinese art. When one examines how this text operates, we find we are not dealing with just the written or spoken language, but also the language of colour, the language of symbolic visual imagery, the language of ritual. Each of these languages is inextricably woven into the Chinese language. My recent work is about how language, text and subtext, together with selective memory, invent an imagined collective cultural past, and so create a context for the individual to construct a narrative of the self. This process is important for the immigrant artist who has to come to terms with and adapt to a new cultural environment.

I have selected several key phrases, Chinese expressions, which I remember from my childhood in Hong Kong. The phrase *hung hung lu lu* (red red green green) is not just a colour scheme. My elders used the phrase frequently when they wished everything to appear visually auspicious, and so, by some magical process, translate into material reality. While these words do not appear as visualised text, the colours are indeed dominant in the work. Another auspicious Chinese character is that for happiness. My use of this, as a central image and in a deliberate act of semiotic reversal, is explained later in the discussion of the red garment, the central work in the exhibition.

A whimsical choice is *mei lan tsu*. Literally, each character means, in order, *beauty* or *beautiful, man* or *male,* and *child.* I remember that in old Cantonese movies the expression was used to mean a male court favourite of the empress, or duchess. But since, I have discovered that more often the male favourite was that of the emperor or duke. Used in a wider sense, it could

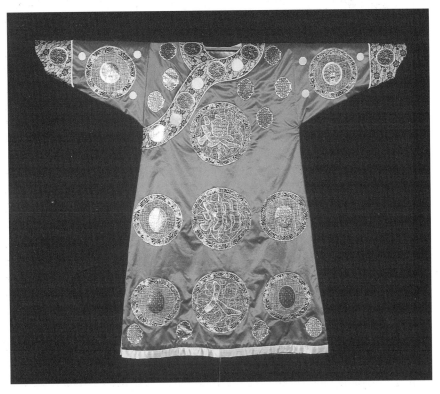

Greg Leong: **Australian (Green) – Pauline** (1998)
embroidery-stitching, beading, soluble plastic bags, computer-imaged print appliqués, silk and acetate satins, synthetic satin lining, fused lace
133 x 156cm (52.5 x 61.5in)

mean a gay man, or a male courtesan. This expression is used very much tongue-in-cheek in *Australian (Gold)*, a fabulous golden vinyl robe with 180 gold plated buttons as decoration. The overall impression of gorgeous 'Chineseness' is, on close inspection, seriously undermined by a repeated decorative image of 'a crotch shot' of a 'hunk' in a rubber cossie, and the golden hand-written text, which loosely translates *mei* as 'beauty' (as in the very Australian 'bewdy, mate!').

My mother, who was born in Australia, was viewed with suspicion by my father's parents, and indeed by any Chinese person who sensed she was different to them – she was an Australian. Her Australianness is pitted against Australianness of quite another ilk in the green costume, *Australian (Green) – Pauline*.

This richly decorated silk garment confronts the viewer with at least two notions of Australian identity. The central image is the three Chinese characters, which together mean (an) Australian (person). The characters are placed on rich see-through embroidered circles. Up close, one discovers that the characters on the front are filled in with multiple images of Pauline Hanson, currently a well-known example of one type of Australian – a politician who actively disapproves of a multicultural immigration policy.[10] On the back of the garment, the characters are made up of images of the artist's Australian born Chinese family. There is yet a third version – a gleeful Asian St. Sebastian (the artist), pierced with arrows, poses against a background of multiple Paulines, in a playful portrait of The Martyred Asian Australian.

In one of the central series of pieces, I stake a claim – *I am Australian*. This statement however is visualised, not in English, but in five Chinese characters. These are affirmations of plurality. To claim to be Australian in a language other than English should send signals to those whose vision of Australia is an exclusively Anglo-Saxon one. Each of these five pieces is contextualised as a camisole. These are articles of Chinese underwear, intimate second skins. They protect the chest and the stomach, and, for the wealthy, camisoles were exquisitely embroidered. Underwear is usually concealed – and yet it is always there fulfilling important tasks while giving sensual comfort.

The Chinese language as used in *Remembering Chinese* is an attempt to reclaim the culture that was never totally mine, growing up in Hong Kong, a British Colony until four years ago. By declaring my Australianness in the Chinese language, a semiotic inversion is achieved. The linguistic sign for 'Australian' is no longer recognisable by exclusively English-speaking Australians.

A second kind of semiotic inversion is created when referencing objects which have a diametrically opposed cultural significance in European culture. Two clear examples of objects or symbols which do not have similar meaning transculturally are the bat and the dragon, both important childhood symbols found on clothing and objects used in Chinese ritual. Other key concepts in the work include colour – the Chinese colours of red, green and gold as contrasted with the Australian colours of green and gold – and Chinese ritual and its relationship with the preceding concepts

The bat is particularly interesting in terms of the inability of the symbol to be translated from a general European cultural context to a specific Asian one without a major shift in our perception of this nocturnal mammal.[11] Far from carrying the stigma that Western mythology has accorded it (night, evil, blindness and so on), the bat is seen by the Chinese as an auspicious symbol.

This motif was commonly used in conjunction with peaches, a symbol of longevity and food of the gods. It was to be found in pairs (particularly auspicious) on the garments of young and old alike. Part of the reason for this is the fluidity of the Chinese language where one sound can carry multiple meanings – and so, Valery Garrett explains, 'the homonym *fu* stands for both "bat" and "happiness", hence the bat is a popular symbol. Five bats shown together signify the Five Blessings: longevity, health, wealth, virtue, and a natural death.'[12]

The bat for me is a powerful multi-faceted symbol. Apart from the obvious irony that the same object can be considered both 'evil' and 'good' by European and Chinese Australians respectively, I also once used to have a clear single understanding of the symbol from childhood and hence the use of the motif becomes a symbolic act of reclamation of my heritage. In addition, and no less important, as a homosexual male, even today, one stands in threat of a most unnatural death by AIDS – the bat as an object then becomes a talisman warding off harm.

The three major works – red, green and gold costumes – all have matching shoes, two pairs each. The three pairs of Manchu platform shoes are set in clear opposition to the three pairs of exquisitely fashioned miniature shoes for bound feet[13] worn by Han Chinese women. The women from the ruling class of Manchus did not have bound feet. When the Manchus took power in the Quing Dynasty (1644–1912), they tried to outlaw, unsuccessfully, the fashion of foot binding. Their women's shoes were markedly different from those of the Han Chinese.[14] The lavishly decorated and ornate styles of shoes and boots of Han women belied the horrible reality of their tortured and deformed feet. On the other hand the Manchu style adopted a raised platform of about 10–15 cm. Although very inconvenient to walk in, these shoes allowed the Manchu woman, already of superior social rank, to physically tower over her Han counterpart. They also caused whoever wore them, to move in such a way as to imitate the swaying gait of bound feet – viewed by the Chinese male as extraordinarily sexually attractive.

While I intend these shoes to speak strongly of (a) the political and socially accepted oppression of minority groups, (b) the fashion expression of superior/inferior social roles, and (c) the aesthetics of minority sexual taste, it would be misleading to impute a strict system of symbolism to my use of objects which references culture/history-specific items of apparel. The resonances of history are seldom clearly explained or are able to be interpreted in only one definitive way.

Hence if a pair of Manchu shoes references elaborate bejewelled footwear of royalty (e.g. Empress Dowager Cixi), the cultural transference strategy I use demands a conceptual and linguistic leap from Chinese Empress Dowager to *Chinese Australian Queen* (a queen of Australia) – or for that matter another sort of queen, Pauline Hanson, the self-proclaimed *Mother of Australia.*

Similarly, in the case of bound feet, for what is considered by the contemporary world as cruelty to women, one might substitute the historical oppression of gay people in Australia on one level and the current undercurrent of blanket racism against Asian Australians on another.

Apart from the *Red Red Green Green* collision with the *Green and Gold*, mentioned earlier as the overriding colour scheme of this body of work, in terms of colour possessing powerful semiotic qualities, red is arguably the most important for the Chinese – certainly the most burdened with recollected meaning for me. My earliest memory of Chinese ritual was of Chinese New Year, during which the all-pervasive colour was red. Auspicious sayings were written in beautiful calligraphy on red paper and posted on walls at home and on the outsides of buildings. *Hung bao* or lucky money[15] – a ceremonial gift of cash – was always wrapped in red paper or latterly put in red envelopes, and called *red packets.* These were available commercially and printed with auspicious characters such as those for longevity, wealth, and, most often, *shuangxi* or double happiness.

All the above trappings of ritual were linked quite significantly with one of the most important Chinese symbols – the dragon. Valery M. Garrett observes that 'female members[16] of the Manchu imperial family wore the dragon robe which often had the double happiness character *shuangxi* included with other symbols.... Later in the dynasty these garments were predominantly in red, reflecting the influence of this auspicious 'Chinese' colour.' I remember vividly how, on important occasions, both my severely traditional paternal grandmother and my mother would wear their *gua* (ceremonial garb), powerfully red and black with embroidered imagery.

We encounter an interesting cultural *impasse* with the use of the dragon symbol. Not only is its Chinese incarnation violently opposite to the attributes bestowed on it by European mythology; as a Chinese sign, its emblematic significance in centuries of strict codes of symbolism, courtly fashion and decorative lore is firmly fixed in the Chinese psyche. The Dragon is perhaps the absolute sign, far from the negative connotations in European pagan as well as Christian mythology. Examples of the latter come quickly to mind: the Archangel Michael defeating the dragon in a symbolic representation of the defeat of darkness by light, an unpleasant and aggressive person is called a dragon and so on.[17]

For the Chinese, the 'dragon represents the highest spiritual power, the divine power of change and transformation; the rhythms of Nature; the law of becoming.... It is ... the masculine yang power ... infinite supernatural power and, on earth, the delegated imperial power, the Emperor.'[18]

The dragon was and still is widely recognised by the Chinese as a former symbol of the emperor. It is less widely known that, as a symbol of male vigour and fertility, it represents the bridegroom on his wedding day. In my work, apart from the obvious transference from Emperor to Empress, and from that to *Queen*, the reference to the dragon is also therefore to the masculine yang powers, symbolised in most cultures by the phallus. So the dragon for me takes on an additional *phallocentric* dimension. While the bride is symbolised by the phoenix motif, the groom is very much in evidence in a bridal garment through the dominant use of the dragon motif.[19]

The ensemble of dragon jacket with a dragon skirt described above – in effect, a woman's 'wedding outfit' – was recycled for wear on any important ceremonial occasion. This ceremonial wear is referenced in my *Australian (Red)* garment. Through it I recall the unpleasantness of a certain type of Chineseness as typified by my paternal grandmother. My mother was singled out amongst her daughters-in-law as the one, because she was foreign-born, to whom the lessons of filial respect had still to be taught. For my grandmother, kneeling and kow-towing on formal occasions such as anniversaries of birth and Chinese New Year were *de rigueur* for daughter-in-law and grandchildren alike. During these thoroughly oppressive occasions both mother-in-law and daughter-in-law wore the dragon ensemble or the commoner's equivalent.

My poor mother! She was born and raised in Sydney and country New South Wales at a time when racial prejudice amongst white Australians was much more freely expressed than it is today. She felt irrevocably rejected as an Asian Australian. Taken back to the 'homeland' she had never known at 14, she was put in the Shanghai School for Overseas Chinese Girls – again separated from the ordinary people of the country.

I remember how she was different from the Hong Kong Chinese when I grew up there. I remember how Westernised she was. She did not seem to think, talk or even dress like other Chinese women in Hong Kong. She prided herself on this difference, and perhaps, as I recall, even nurtured a stance of superiority over and perhaps a secret disdain for the locally born Chinese.

Many years later, when I came to live in Australia as an adult, I was shocked to discover how my childhood and early teenage perception of my mother's western alienness in Hong Kong had been transmogrified by some unfathomable transcultural process. She was, *is*, equally a stranger in the country of her birth! Within a white Australian context, how very *Chinese* my mother now seems, as she nurses a huge life-long hurt that only victims of racial unkindness can understand.[20]

The red garment (see colour plate 6), the one that stands for luck and all manner of auspiciousness, works in several ways. In the simplest and least obscure reading – and in keeping with the cultural transferral strategy used in much of my work – it is the *yin* (feminine – bridal) expression of my *yang* (masculinity – the dragon). In other words, to claim to be the bride rather than the groom, to want to ritually dress like my mother and grandmother rather than my father or his father, is an inversion of my masculinity.

On another level, it is a remembrance of my childhood through a predominant colour – red. These also are the robes – or similar ones – which I remember my mother and grandmother wearing when they were at their most ritualistically Chinese. Whether or not the *gua* (ceremonial costume) worn by my mother and grandmother were in fact exact versions of *mang ao* and *mang chu*, the dragon jacket and skirt have become very firm constructs of my memory.

But most poignantly for me it is a commemoration of the plight of my mother, a victim of a double cultural displacement, of a historical white Australian racism and of the no less prejudicial, rigid structures of Chinese ritual and familial relations. And so – returning to the use of common Chinese linguistic signifiers – I have referenced the popular auspicious symbol for Double Happiness (*shuangxi*), used on all celebratory occasions, in the red garment.

Greg Leong: 'xuangbei'
(double sorrow), detail of
**Australian (Red) – My
Mother's Bridal Ensemble**
silk brocade, polyester satin,
fused lace, screen-print
25cm (10in) diameter

I have paired this with a linguistic invention – a semiotic inversion – by creating a pair of characters denoting Double Sorrow (*shuangbei*) – a transgressive action of some emotional power for the Chinese, as we would never willingly invoke unhappiness for ourselves through the use of inauspicious symbols, language or ritual. Here it is to acknowledge that the double happiness of being both Asian and Australian, and of being both gay and Chinese Australian, is also the source for double sorrow.

As I have arrived at an age when one's story can disappear with the loss of parents and other elderly relatives, the desire to retrieve the past becomes a necessity, a luxury that must be enjoyed before it is no longer available. Through the story of my mother, a Chinese Australian born during a racially intolerant time, I have started to consider the complex facets of personal cultural/sexual identity against the larger canvas of an elusive

'Australian National Identity'. I have resorted to *remembering*, and relied on memory's unfailing selectivity to re-order and isolate events and so form some version of a personal narrative in order to make sense of the present.

Notes

1. This paper is based on the artist statement from the catalogue of my 1999–2000 touring solo exhibition, *Remembering Chinese*, and on the subsequent paper, 'Remembering Chinese' in Helen Gilbert, Tseen Khoo and Jacqueline Lo (eds.), *Diaspora: Negotiating Asian-Australia*, Queensland University Press, St. Lucia, 2000, pp. 58–68.
2. Claire Roberts (ed.), *Evolution & Revolution – Chinese Dress 1700s – 1990s*, p. 9.
3. Ibid. p. 9.
4. Joanne Entwistle and Elizabeth Wilson, 'The Body Clothed', in *Addressing the Century – pp.* 110–111.
5. Glynis Jones: 'Outrageous! Costume & Confections' *in Absolutely Mardi Gras – Costume and Design of the Sydney Gay & Lesbian Mardi Gras*, p. 35 and p. 49.
6. Nikos Papastergiadis, *Dialogues in the Diasporas – Essays and conversations on Cultural Identity*, p. x.
7. See Diana Giese, *Astronauts, Lost Souls & Dragons – Voices of today's Chinese Australians in conversation with Diana Giese*, p. 3. She distinguishes several categories, including established migrant families, people who came under education schemes, refugees, and more recent arrivals.
8. In 1901, the Federation of Australia enabled a federal law to be enacted making it difficult for people of Asian origin to settle or migrate to Australia. This was the infamous 'White Australia Policy'. In contrast, from the late nineteen-sixties there was, until the current government under John Howard, a multicultural immigration policy. It has been argued that the migration of different peoples to Australia has made a beneficial contribution to the development of a new Australian Identity. Labour's multicultural push and the era of political correctness ended with the advent of the Howard Liberal Government in 1994 and the Pauline Hanson (and her One Nation Party) phenomenon.
9. The use of text, especially the embroidered *shou* (longevity) character of funerary garments, was not an uncommon practice.
10. In her parliamentary maiden speech, 10 September 1996, Pauline Hanson concluded that a 'truly multicultural country can never be strong or united'.
11. For a clear example of the difficulties of cross-cultural translation, see the entry on the bat from J.C. Cooper's *Dictionary of Symbolic and Mythological Animals*, pp. 14–15, in which the bat is seen variously as evil (western folklore, the Old Testament, Buddhism), unlucky or unclean (Japan, Maori New Zealand) in some traditions and, in others, sacred (Aboriginal myth, several parts of Africa), lucky (China, ancient Egypt) and an acceptable food (Assyria and Africa).
12. Valery M. Garrett, *A Collector's Guide to Chinese Dress Accessories*, p. 21.
13. Foot binding began sometime between the end of the Tang Dynasty (907 AD) and the Song Dynasty (960 AD) and continued until early last century. See Garrett, Ibid. pp. 92–93.
14. See Garrett, Ibid. pp. 135–146, and Claire Roberts, Ibid.p.37.
15. *Hung bao* – literal translation, red packet. One of the rituals of Chinese New Year was the giving of 'lucky money' to children, social inferiors, and so on.
16. Valery Garrett, *Chinese Clothing: An Illustrated Guide*, p. 133.

17. See J.C. Cooper, Ibid. pp. 55–6.
18. Cooper, Ibid. p. 56.
19. See Garrett, 1997, p. 23.
20. This history is screen-printed onto the panels of the border of the red wedding jacket.

Remembering Toba Tek Singh:
A video installation by Nalini Malani

Victoria Lynn

In a seminal book on Indian dress and identity, Emma Tarlo argues that 'the problem of what to wear is formulated within the framework of the specific historical development of a culture. In India this problem has for the past century been inextricably linked to the colonial encounter and its after-effects.'[1] Uncut cloth is described variously by Tarlo as a political, moral, ritual and economic symbol in India.

This chapter focuses on a video installation by Nalini Malani, one of India's most prominent contemporary artists. Her work has been exhibited internationally in Australia, India, the United Kingdom, Denmark, Korea and Japan. She works in a variety of media, including painting, video, watercolour, artist's books, installation and performance. Of central importance is her concern with the effects of globalisation on the local ecology and on the female body. As a member of India's intellectual community, Nalini Malani is conversant with arguments about identity formation in the Indian context. She is also part of a much larger community which has the choice to change clothes (jeans, shalwar kamiz, saris) from one day to the next. She consciously presents her work in the context of the India/Pakistan Partition of 1947 which had a direct bearing on her own family. Malani's family had to move from Pakistan to India when she was a child. Nearly 500,000 people lost their lives when the Indian subcontinent was divided on political and religious grounds. Between 12 and 14 million people were left homeless. 60 million of the 95 million Muslims (one in four Indians) became Pakistanis: 35 million stayed in India, the largest number of Muslims in a non-Muslim state.[2] As Rita Menon says:

'Partition, almost uniquely, is the one event in our recent history in which familial recall and its encoding are a significant factor in any general reconstruction of it. In a sense, it is the collective memory of thousands of displaced families on both sides of the border that have imbued a rather innocuous word – partition – with its dreadful meaning: a people violently displaced, a country divided. Partition: a metaphor for irreparable loss'.[3]

Documentary films about Partition show a line of people passing each other across new borders. This is a recurrent image in Nalini Malani's practice.

Nalini Malani's work asserts itself metaphorically and symbolically over and across the dominant symbols of the Indian state. The use of the sari has recently surfaced as such a symbol in her video installation *Remembering Toba Tek Singh*. In this complex art work, the synchronous rhythms of clothing, gesture, body and voice are integrated with the unfolding and repeated references to displacement, migration, immigration and war: the turbulence of conflict. Elizabeth Wilson suggests that dress 'links the biological body to the social being, and public to private ... dress is the frontier between the self and the not self'.[4] Nalini Malani activates this frontier by transforming the sari into a performing entity that is tossed and tied between two contemporary women on the screen.

Remembering Toba Tek Singh is Nalini Malani's first video installation. It was created in 1998 and has since featured in exhibitions in India, the Netherlands, Australia and Korea.[5] The work consists of four large projections that occupy three walls (the central image is a split screen combination of two video projections). On the floor are twelve metal trunks with their lids slightly ajar. Inside the trunks are video monitors, face up, along with fragments of uncut Indian cloth and bedding. The floor is black and shiny and reflects the images on the walls.

The title of this work is based on a short story by Saadat Hasan Manto and part of the story is played as a sound track within the installation. Manto is a well-known writer in both Pakistan and India and the story is a common text for high school children. It tells the tale of Bishen Singh, who was in a hospital for the psychically disturbed during the Partition of India and Pakistan in 1947. At the time, Muslim patients were to be transferred to Pakistan, and Hindu and Sikh patients to India. Along with other patients he was moved to the border from which he was to be transported, but Bishen Singh refused to be moved from the centre line in no-man's land. He stood there and died. For him, the two countries had no meaning in his reality; he could not imagine a border.

The central screens in the installation show archival images of the American bombs 'Fat Boy' and 'Little Man' that killed millions of people in Hiroshima and Nagasaki during World War II. These are superimposed over Nalini Malani's single cell animation drawings. Along with the two screens on either edge of the installation, the central image displays black

Nalini Malani: **Remembering Toba Tek Singh** (1998), detail
video installation

and white sequences of two Indian women, dressed in simple modern clothing, playing with the chiffon sari. These large projections are synchronised in the space so that the two women are relating to one another in a very real way across the four video projections. They literally throw the sari back and forth, fold it together, unfold it and share either end of it. They variously tie it around their waists, fold it into slim concertina-ed sections and cover their heads and bodies. The women wear unembellished black T-shirts and black pants. At times, they roll towards and away from one another across the white floor. Their facial expressions range from an uncompromising stare, through a playfulness to estrangement. The two screens at either end of the installation are exactly opposite one another. With slow, careful gestures, each woman holds opposite ends of the sari and begins to fold the long diaphanous cloth. They are unable to touch or to complete their folding in our real space because they are, metaphorically, trapped in the frame of the screen.

The images on the monitors in the trunks depict people torn away from their homelands, crossing borders, rioting and suffering. These are the kinds of trunks in which we pack all our worldly possessions. Many of these video images are taken from archival material from several countries. All is in flux: victims of Hiroshima, refugees in Bosnia, lines of people crossing the border of Pakistan and India, riots in Mumbai in 1992–3 in the midst of Hindu-Muslim fundamentalist tension.[6] In one image, a western woman is giving birth, in another, an Indian woman explains that, after the nuclear testing in her region, her son was born with a deformed ear. In a different sequence on the larger screen, one of the women presses her face against a transparent surface, transforming it into a mutated image.

In the period 1994–6, Nalini Malani painted a series of images of ungendered *Mutants*. Commenting on her *Mutants*, she has said, 'whatever a person goes through in his or her life, suppose it was registered on the skin, what would be the feel of that?' Skin is not only constituted by culture in this installation, it is also mutated, like the environment, by technologies such as nuclear testing, genetic farming and the damning of waterways. Malani has said that 'women are not the decision makers of this destructive enterprise called nuclear testing; indeed they are the sufferers and the victims, as it is they who will give birth to deformed babies'. The metal trunks, then, carry the stories of people left homeless by war and mutated by environmental destruction. They also show fragments from various documentaries and a simple row of clouds against a blue sky, which offer the only peaceful image in this collection of suffering.

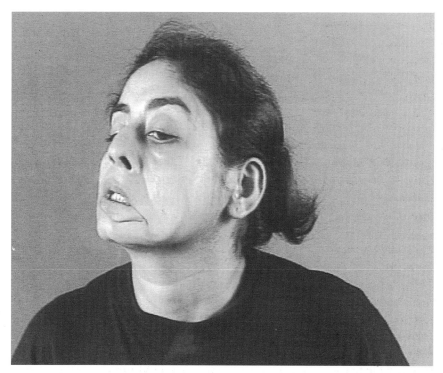

Nalini Malani: **Remembering Toba Tek Singh** (1998), detail
video installation

Nalini Malani's concerns with the plight of women in contemporary India may be further understood with reference to comments made by the Australian feminist writer, Elizabeth Grosz. 'The body is not opposed to culture, a resistant throwback to a natural past; it is itself cultural, the cultural product. The very question of the ontological status of biology, the openness of organic processes to cultural intervention, transformation, or even production, must be explored'.[7] And further, 'The surface of the body is in a particularly privileged position to receive information and excitations from both the interior and exterior of the organism.... The information provided by the surface of the skin is both endogenous and exogenous, active and passive, receptive and expressive'.[8] In *Remembering Toba Tek Singh*, skin is mutated by the adverse effects of nuclear testing in one image, distorted by birth in another, and wilfully transformed by one of the performers in a third video sequence as she presses her face against glass. In this work, female skin (as a metaphor for female identity) is constituted from both within and without, organically and culturally.

Remembering Toba Tek Singh was made in response to the nuclear tests in India on 11 May 1998. The tests created a tension between India and Pakistan, especially in Kashmir. As the central screen shows bombs dropping over cities, and billowing smoke fills the screen, the two women (who Malani has likened to the chorus in Greek tragedies) make incessant but futile attempts at folding the sari. Each poetic configuration of the sari takes on metaphoric connotations: the veil, the mushroom cloud, and nature, earth.

The sari has been subject to various interpretations in texts about the sub-continent. Some indication of its complex signification can be understood from art historical studies which identify one of the earliest depictions of a woman wearing a sari as a Shunga period sculpture from 100BC. Sociological studies show that today sari production comprises 25.5% of all textile production in India.[9] Textile histories reveal that saris vary in length from 3 to 8 metres (10 to 26 feet) and that they can have everyday value as well as ritual value depending on their design and the occasion of their transaction.[10] The sari also has its own history within the politics of display, occupying a central role as an object of museum classification in India.

The tension apparent in *Remembering Toba Tek Singh* is the result of Partition, colonisation and the ongoing conflicts between religious fundamentalist groups. India's own textile industry has a history within this same colonialist context. Uncut cloth has shuttled between the United Kingdom and the sub-continent as an object, a design and a concept. There are numerous examples of mutations in design as a result of this trade. For example, under the domination of the British East India Company, established in the eighteenth century, textiles from India were studied by manufacturers in Manchester and in the west of Scotland who imitated the Indian cloth, exporting their own version back to India and thus threatening local industries. As designs were transformed (consider the similarities between the Paisley shawl and the Kashmiri shawl), the ability to identify tradition through cloth became increasingly complex and fluid.

A similar kind of textile history is also the central concern of the work of British artist Yinka Shonibare, whose renowned sculpture *Mr and Mrs Andrews without their Heads* (1998) shows the two well known figures from Gainsborough's painting, dressed in so-called 'African' cloth.[11] Shonibare has shown how identity is miscommunicated and misplaced through dress. In the nineteenth century, Indonesian batik was taken back to the Netherlands by the Dutch colonialists where it was produced by the Dutch and then imitated by the cotton trade in Manchester which then re-exported batik designs to British colonies, including West Africa. West

Africans learnt the techniques of printing and design and, in the spirit of independence, began to produce the cloth in their own country. Subsequently, West African immigrants to Britain came to associate these designs with their own identity (unaware of their origin) wearing them as a symbol of their indigeneity. This then created a demand for 'authentic' African cloth within Britain, which required African cloth to be (re-) imported to Britain.

The association of an indigenous textile industry with a national independence has had many political, aesthetic and industrial manifestations in India. Varied cultural, bureaucratic and political groups in Indian society have tried to keep the textile industry afloat. For example, in the early decades of the twentieth century Mahatma Ghandi promoted spinning as a political, economic and moral symbol. Often the spun thread was to be exchanged for woven cloth. Indians were encouraged to weave khadi (hand-spun, hand-woven cloth) as well as wear it in the form of shirts, pyjamas and 'Ghandi' caps for men and khadi saris for women, as an assertion of Indian independence. Earlier in the century, Ananda K. Coomaraswamy promoted the idea that all Indians revert to 'Indian' dress in order to achieve a religious-artistic ideal,[12] while after Independence the Indian Handicrafts Board, established in 1952, encouraged the production and appreciation of Indian handicrafts.[13]

Nalini Malani, like Shonibare, does not promote a fixed identity through dress. Rather than tying the sari to an essential Indian identity, the implication at the heart of Malani's work is that such associations are nostalgic, and halt the growth of culture over time. Her installation reinforces the multiple crossovers between symbol and material caused by colonialism and Partition. A telling moment in one of the smaller video sequences shows a young man shouting, 'Go and wear a sari' (see colour plate 2). He is one of a crowd during the riots between Hindus and Muslims in Mumbai in the early 1990s and the scene is from a documentary film by Anand Patwardhan, entitled *Father, Son and Holy War*. We can only guess at his meaning, but in the context of Malani's installation, his comment comes to be associated with a religious and political conservatism that insists the sari be identified with a specific role for women.

Nalini Malani's installation shows that the contemporary concept of 'India' is in itself a construction born of colonialism. In *Remembering Toba Tek Singh*, the performance of the sari resists being seen as a fixed symbol of the 'Indian' or 'Indian woman'. Such identifications would orientalise and simplify the sari's broad and changing significance. Given this complexity, it is well worth recalling Ashis Nandy's comment that 'there can be no such thing as "the Indian", since the West is now everywhere, within the West and outside; in structures and in minds'.[14]

In his studies of the changes in music across the 'Black' Atlantic, Paul Gilroy has asked, 'how do we think critically about artistic products and aesthetic codes which, though they may be traceable back to one distinct location, have been changed, either by the passage of time or by their displacement, relocation, or dissemination through networks of communication and cultural exchange?'[15] In *Remembering Toba Tek Singh*, the sari is not a piece of clothing, for the women are already clothed. The sari is being exchanged between two women. Is it being tossed from Pakistan to India? From one sister to another? From friend to friend? Its flow and shift through the space of the installation attests to its roaming meanings within India (it is literally untied), and also asserts it as a performance object and symbol. In this way, the sari is changed and changing through the very modalities that Gilroy identifies: displacement, relocation and networks of cultural exchange.

The chiffon sari is regarded as a modern sari in India, and has been made popular by the Bollywood film industry.[16] Malani's sari is covered with flowers. While flowers have a symbolic role in both Hindu and Buddhist iconography, their use on a sari of this type is purely decorative. They could be the Buta and Buti, motifs commonly found in certain saris depicting groups of flowers against a plain background, but their place in this installation pulls the floral arrangements away from the history of floral symbolism in the sari and the Bollywood context, to a more general sense of nature – the billowing movement of the cloth echoes both the organic lines of nature that are being destroyed by global environmental disaster and the atomic clouds of destruction that are visible in the video projections. As the American artist Ann Hamilton showed in her work *Bearings* (1996), billowing silk organza cloth that is set into motion can have endless associations with female dress, nature, fertility, the veil and states of motion and fluidity. Nothing is fixed in Nalini Malani's performance: the sari misbehaves.

In an earlier watercolour book entitled *The Degas Suite*, Malani painted images of Indian women over photocopied drawings she had made after the work of the French Impressionist Edgar Degas. She has commented that in Degas' imagery, women are depicted as the 'drudge'.[17] She has also drawn on the work of Picasso, Goya, Titian, Cranach, the Indian Kalighat painters and the early Indian modernist painter, Ravi Verma. Malani worked with watercolour over her own versions of Degas' drawings which she reproduced in multiple photocopies. In her hands, the female figure comes to consider her own body and her own sexuality. One female figure, for instance, is cradled by another woman's arm. Rather than depicting women as objects to be admired and consumed, Malani's watercolours bring together Degas' women with Indian women in an active and animated environment. They appear to be in a watery dialogue with one another. She transforms Degas' images, while also allowing their beauty to filter through and gives a voice to the voiceless women of Degas' drawings and to their silent allure, an active subjectivity.[18] The translucency of the chiffon sari is not unlike these watercolour images that filter another reality through their own, freeing one image by imbuing it with others.

Though the video images do not form a complete circle around the metal trunks in the centre of *Remembering Toba Tek Singh*, there is an implied continuity of gesture between the screens. At one point, the two women each appear twice, and the sari is tossed from the older to the younger to the older to the younger and in reverse across four screens. This strong performative element creates a spatial metaphor in the work. The artist has created an architectural site for her moving images with its own pattern, layout and construction. Perhaps it is also an archaeological site; a layering of media images and performances of conflict, displacement, environmental disaster and textile memories. For instance, the textiles that spill out from the tin trunks – old bedding, torn pieces of uncut cloth, brightly coloured yet soiled pieces of silk and cotton – recall a lost period of stability. Within this formal context, the free flowing sari in the videos becomes a more potent symbol.

This installation presents the cleaving of countries and the irrational, inhuman use of war technology. The lulling, rhythmic gestures of the two modern women playing with a sari covered in images of flowers offer a resistant voice in the midst of a layering of irreconcilable horrors. The short story *Toba Tek Singh* is about a patient who does not understand the difference between reality and fiction. He sees a world that has slipped into madness, sickness and division and he takes refuge in a no-man's land between modern borders of cultural displacement, an in-between space that the two women in the installation also, metaphorically, embrace. There are many layered realities in India, and Malani offers an image of Indian women which is in marked contrast to conventional associations with the 'motherland': the metonymic connections and displacements that cross the notion of woman as nation as Hindu Goddess as Bollywood movie star. Stuart Hall has suggested that in contemporary Britain 'race is the modality in which class is lived', while Paul Gilroy expands on this by contending that 'gender is the modality in which race is lived'.[19] Reflecting the complexity of social encounters within India, the relationships between gender, identity, class, textile and the female body in *Remembering Toba Tek Singh* are brought together in a fluid and shifting zone, one that suggests that political, economic and environmental imperialism is the modality through which women live and give birth. This is a destabilising zone that flickers with as much memorable intensity and randomness as the moving image itself.

Notes

1. Tarlo, *Clothing Matters*, p. 330.
2. Menon, Ritu and Bhasin, Kamla, *Borders & Boundaries: Women in India's Partition*, p.4.
3. Menon, *Borders & Boundaries*, p. xi.
4. Wilson, *Adorned in Dreams: Fashion and Modernity*, pp. 2–3.
5. Worldwide Video Festival, Amsterdam, 1998; Prince of Wales Museum, Mumbai, India, 1999; *Voiceovers, The Fifth Guinness Contemporary Art Project*, Art Gallery of New South Wales, Sydney, 1999; Kwanju Biennale, Kwanju, Korea, 2000. The work is now in the collection of the Queensland Art Gallery, Brisbane, Australia.
6. While a sensitivity to socio-political issues is by no means new in modern Indian art, the rise of religious fundamentalism in the wake of the destruction of the Muslim temple in Ayodhya in 1990 has been of paramount importance to artists' thinking in recent years. The violence, fear and fierce energy of the riots in 1992–3 is often cited as a catalyst for a change of direction in the work of contemporary artists. Some have chosen to explore the relationship between spiritual myths and violence. Others have eschewed any hint of specific religious references in their work. Allusions to political threat have also crept into the art works. In addition, many artists, musicians, writers, actors and filmmakers have been actively involved in an organisation called SAHMAT, the Sadfar Hashmi Memorial Trust, set up to emphasise the importance of peace, upholding the values of secularism and cultural pluralism. Exhibitions, performances and concerts are held across India on a regular basis in order to raise awareness of these issues.
7. Grosz, *Volatile Bodies. Toward a Corporeal Feminism*, p. 23.
8. Grosz, *Volatile Bodies*, pp. 35–36.
9. Lynton, *The Sari Styles Patterns History Techniques*, pp. 11–12.
10. Askari, N. and Arthur, Liz, *Uncut Cloth: Saris, Shawls and Sashes*, p. 39.
11. Thomas Gainsborough (1727–88) *Mr and Mrs Andrews*, National Gallery, London.
12. Coomaraswamy, *Art and Swadeshi*.
13. Tarlo, *Clothing Matters*.
14. Ashis Nandy, *The Intimate Enemy: Loss and Recovery of Self Under Colonialism*, p. xi.
15. Gilroy, *The Black Atlantic Modernity and Double Consciousness*, p. 80.
16. Lynton, *The Sari Styles*, p. 11. The Bollywood film industry is the largest in the world, boasting more film productions than Hollywood in Los Angeles. It often paves the way for new fashions, music and social behaviour in India. Some Bollywood movie stars are worshipped with religious fervour.
17. Correspondence with the author, 14 August 1999.
18. Malani's references to Degas are just one example of the many ways in which Indian artists have transformed European modernism in order to create an independent form of modernism within India.
19. Gilroy, *Black Atlantic*, p. 85.

Glossary of Terms

Gujarati: Gujarat is a state in India distinguished for its textiles.

Shalwar kamiz: a form of Indian dress for women that includes a knee-length, long-sleeved tunic top and loose trousers.

Buta and Buti: Small (buti) and large (buta) flowers, sprigs and bushes in a floating design against a plain background, found in saris. Floral buti first appeared in the lungis (draped clothing) in classical Indian bronzes from the seventh to the ninth century. (Lynton, *The Sari Styles*, p. 171.)

Embroidering the Motherland: The Fabric of Palestinian National Identity

Tina Sherwell

While studying textiles at Goldsmiths College I began to explore the question of Palestinian identity. This arose out of an inquiry into my own identity, being of both British and Palestinian descent. The work I created during that time explored the map as a representational form which could be deconstructed through textile art. The language of textiles – in particular pinning, darning and seaming, provided a way of expressing the history that had fragmented the land of Palestine and that had consequently created a nostalgia for a lost homeland. The activity of darning, patching and seaming layers of maps together became acts of preservation, yet the works suggested that these acts could not restore the plenitude of the lost homeland, for the maps were awkwardly held together and the fragments were inconsistent. With no memory of my own of Palestine and not having been raised with narratives of a lost homeland, I took on a nostalgia for something I had not known but was lost to me.

Looking back in retrospect, I can trace from my textile practice my pre-occupation with the way Palestinian identities are constructed and preserved, and in which re-presentations of the past occupy a central place. One of the ways this preservation and re-creation of Palestinian identity takes place is through textiles, in particular embroidery, both in its creation and its re-presentation. For it is the traditional embroidery patterns of the former Palestinian peasant woman that have become central to the vocabulary of Palestinian identity.

Why is it that this element from women's culture has become such a popular symbol and what does its popularity suggest about national perceptions of the role of women and their bodies? By exploring the popularity of embroidery which has come to function as a way of signaling Palestinian national identity, I am able to take apart the meanings that textiles are embellished with and the way they have been used to express different ideas about national identity. Embroidery in particular can create an image of the past and of a lost homeland.

What I would like to suggest is that textiles are one of the spaces through which the homeland is gendered, and articulate the way gender divisions are constructed in the national discourse.

Land and Identity

To understand the relationship between textiles and images of the Palestinian homeland one needs to understand the central place land holds in Palestinian identity. The land of Palestine has long occupied the European imagination for it was perceived as an empty land and often represented as such in visual forms such as photography in the 19th century.[1] When its inhabitants were acknowledged, they were represented as descendants of Biblical forefathers, yet seen as people who were inherently backward and had neglected the cultivation and preservation of the Holy Land.[2] What observers ignored were the growing cities and the rich cultural life that had grown up. I raise this point for it is important in the context of understanding international support for the Zionist project of establishing a national homeland for the Jewish people during the first half of the last century.

Palestine already held a place in European consciousness and the image of Palestine that had been cultivated in visual forms, literature, travel accounts and political discourses facilitated the Zionist project. Britain received the mandate from the United Nations to govern Palestine after the dissolution of the Ottoman Empire at the end of World War I and it was the British who actively supported the founding of a Jewish State. Antagonism between local Palestinian inhabitants and the new Jewish settlers led to the withdrawal of Britain and to the outbreak of war between the two communities.[3] In the war of 1948, Israel established itself on 77% of the land of Palestine.[4] As a consequence, half of the population, some 700,000 people, became refugees.[5]

Palestine was removed from the map and its remaining terrains became the West Bank (which fell under Jordanian rule) and The Gaza Strip (which fell under Egyptian administration). This was the status quo until 1967 when Israel seized these territories, placing them under Israeli occupation.

The conflict between Palestinians and Israelis is primarily a conflict over land in which two national communities lay claim to the same terrain. Hence each respective community has focused its national discourse on articulations of their bond with the land. The two communities, however, have not been equally placed in the conditions they have for creating identity representations. Israel has at its disposal a state apparatus which includes an education system, army training, museums, a tourist industry and so forth, with which to facilitate its representation of the land. The Palestinians do not have similar institutions. Rather, they have had to contend with the fact that their population is not located in one geographical terrain and that they had no central representative authority residing in the Occupied Territories until the establishment of the Palestinian National Authority when the Occupied Territories became autonomous regions in 1994/1995. Significantly, Palestinians have also had to confront the suppression of their national-political identity, both in the host countries of the Arab World where they found themselves refugees, and in Israel and the Occupied Territories. For Israel, in particular, articulations of Palestinian identity posed a threat to their own national narrative, for the State did not recognise the Palestinians as a national community with rights to the same terrain as Israel. It is in these contexts that contemporary Palestinian national culture has evolved – one in which, as I have suggested, the articulation of a relationship to the land is central.

The significance of land, and what colours its representation among Palestinians, is that the land of Palestine has been lost. Thus for Palestinians, Palestine is constituted through memories and histories expressed on a personal and communal level. These memories have been pivotal in the process of identity formation of Palestinians both inside and outside the Occupied Territories. Recollections of the past have been elaborated in numerous forms. A rich oral tradition, for example, has insured that several generations of refugees carry the memories and stories of the villages of their parents and grandparents, and village dialects that no longer exist can be heard in the speech of today's Palestinians. Family alliances, rites of passage, folklore dances, theatre, literature, embroidery are all arenas for the reconstruction of the past, and some of these have become national traditions in their own right.

Processes of remembering and holding on to the past become embedded into holding on to one's identity in the face of antagonism, and it is worth noting the political dimension of memory in the Palestinian context, for memory functions as a resistance strategy.

For Palestinians living on land that was once Palestine, the continual narration to each other, and to visitors, of what the landscape was previously like serves as a way of holding onto places that once existed. Similarly, changes to the landscape – the opening of new roads, building works and so forth – are noted, for Palestinians understand that these geographical and spatial transformations culminate in the erasure of their history.

For me, the Palestinian costume is one of the elements of the past that has been identified as a site for the articulation of social memory. I will argue that certain aspects of the costume have taken on a heightened significance. The costume is valued as a symbol of national identity because, I believe, it arose from a tradition derived from the land, being part of the dress of the peasantry. Its central significance comes from the fact that because each region had its own dress with specific traditions of colour, embroidery and shape, the dresses have become a way of mapping and reconstituting the lost homeland. They have become the remains of places that no longer exist. This has served to subsume the other identities that they represented including family wealth and female sexuality. The former was represented through the density of stitchwork, which consumed expensive thread, and the labour time of a female of the family.[6] A woman's sexuality was represented by a long opening at the front of the dress, which is no longer found in contemporary versions.

It is in keeping with the idea of how elements of the past are re-presented that we can begin to deconstruct the popularity of Palestinian embroidery which stems from the tradition of the peasant costume. I would like to argue that the continual circulation and reproduction of this tradition of the past can be understood by the fact that embroidery, and in particular the embroidered women's costume, is a site for the convergence of ideas in which multiple identifications can co-exist within the rubric of national identity.

Peasant Identity and National Identity

I have suggested the centrality of land to the construction of Palestinian identity. This identification has been elaborated through two important signifiers – the village and the peasantry – and the context in which the Palestinian costume and embroidery were made. The peasantry were taken up as a national signifier for articulating the Palestinian historic and continuous tie to the land. The peasantry's former Resistance to change, scorned in the past[7], was re-interpreted as a form of steadfastness. The peasantry became the embodiment of *sumud* – steadfastness – which was the political resistance strategy adapted by the Palestinians of the Occupied Territories in the late 1970s and early 1980s. The image of the peasantry was also significant in binding the Palestinians to the land and to place.[8] This was important in the context of a population which was dispersed in different locations and of which thousands had lost their homes and community. Thus the image of the peasantry was a way of countering the experience of exile, estrangement and of being a refugee.

Through identification with the peasantry, Palestinians were able to articulate the fact that they were from a particular place. Peasant identity functioned as a way of representing the roots and origins of the nation – the 'essence' of Palestinian identity. In their different identities, many of which were no longer grounded in life on the land, Palestinians could tie themselves back to the land of Palestine. This functioned in a way described by Stuart Hall: 'such images offer a way of imposing an imaginary coherence on the experience of dispersal and fragmentation which is the history of all enforced diasporas'.[9] From the position of the peasantry in the national discourse we can understand why their material culture is central to the vocabulary of national identity and has become infused with national symbolism.

Along with the peasantry, 'the village' has also been appropriated as a space for the national imagination. Stephen Daniels explains the importance certain landscapes come to occupy in a national psyche: 'Landscapes, whether focusing on single monuments or framing stretches of scenery, provide visual shape: they picture the nation. As exemplar of the moral order and aesthetic harmony, particular landscapes achieve the status of national icons'.[10]

In Palestinian literature, theatre, paintings and popular culture, the image of the village is predominantly one of a harmonious community which lives upon a land rich in agricultural produce and provides for all. The utopic vision projected in these images recasts the past of the peasantry, where internal conflicts between villagers, poverty and the pressures of taxation and conscription to the Ottoman army are absent. My aim is not to suggest a binary opposition between the images and historic information about the past since they are all forms of re-presentation. What is significant is the ideas that are imparted in the re-presentation of the past of the village and the lives of the peasantry.

The construction of Palestine as a past utopia reads not only as a re-presentation of the past but significantly also as a projection of the future state. In images of the village and the peasantry the future is seen as a return to the past – a past emptied of its former hardships and one in which contemporary estrangement from the landscape and transformations of the landscape are erased. Similarly the social order of the nation is envisaged in a way which utilises a previous social formation to create the larger, anonymous and more recently invented social formation – the nation, which Benedict Anderson has described as the imagined community.[11]

The structure of this social order is revealed for example in a painting by Sliman Mansour entitled *The Village Awakens* (see colour plate 1).

In this painting members of the community engage in harvesting, fruit-picking, stone carving and so forth. The image is one of self-sufficiency and productivity. The painting can be read as a national allegory, for the village is represented as a microcosm of a society in which every person has a designated role contributing to the life and productivity of the village. Repeated on a grand scale, this system provides a prototype for the nation. The painting was produced during the intifada, a period during which Palestinians actively created home industries and adopted a strategy of non-compliance with the Israeli occupation as a form of resistance. In this way they attempted to separate themselves from the occupation.[12]

Significantly, the painting reveals the position of women in the social order, for 'woman' is represented by the figure of a giant peasant woman from whom the villagers march forth and her central role is reproducer of the nation. The giant scale of the woman also means she takes on an architectural and landscape quality, suggesting an interchangeability between women's bodies and the land, and thereby revealing the gendering of the homeland. It is noteworthy that the woman is identified by her peasant dress, which serves to mark her body as national territory. A series of popular postcards of historic sites in Palestine include young women posing in traditional dress, emphasising the association between women and the nation's landscape.

In national discourses and conflicts the spaces of women's bodies have become a terrain in which the conflict is fought out. Since women are represented as the reproducers of the nation, their bodies are often targeted by the enemy and this has been the case with Palestinian women.[13] Palestinians and Israelis have also engaged in a demographic war.[14] The high fertility rate among Palestinians should not, however, be understood solely in terms of national obligation, but as having its roots in peasant family structures and the idea that children provide protection for parents in old age. The imaging of women in reproductive roles reinforces traditional values and makes producing children a patriotic activity.

In Palestinian art, the majority of women are represented in the traditional embroidered costume, emphasing the relationship between their bodies and the space of the nation. Such ideas of women's bodies was evident in a political communique distributed in leaflet form during the

Intifada which called upon women to celebrate the declaration of independence in the following way:

'Palestinian flags will be flown in the cities, villages and refugee camps of our Palestinian state and the women of our people will adorn themselves in Palestinian dresses'.[15]

Thus it is women who are called upon to display the identity of the nation. Women in peasant costume were represented as the 'privileged bearers of cultural authenticity'.[16] They were seen as preserving traditions that stemmed from the land through activities such as cooking traditional foods, embroidering and harvesting. The imaging of women in such roles and in activities of child rearing in popular culture and the visual arts cultivated an idea of the homeland as motherland, and it is through the representation of the peasant woman's activities that the qualities of the homeland are revealed.

Images of women's domestic and nurturing work created an image of the homeland as a place of comfort and security, a gratifying place, in which the subject's emotional and bodily needs are cared for. Imaging Palestine as a motherland creates an image of the homeland as a domestic utopia, while the loss of the homeland becomes a severance from the mother figure and so the desire to return to the homeland is elaborated as a desire to return to infancy and innocence. This is eulogised in many Palestinian poems such as the work of Mahmoud Darwish, who wrote in *Give Birth to Me Once Again*: 'Give birth to me again so I can drink the country's milk from you and remain a little boy in your arms, remain a little boy forever. I have seen many things, mother I have seen. Give birth to me again so you can hold me in your hands'.[17]

Living Traditions

The abundant representation and reproduction of embroidery in Palestinian culture can be understood as a manifestation of the idea of the homeland as domestic utopia. Embroidery patterns can be found on a whole range of objects for the home including mirror frames, stools, table mats and runners, cushions, chairs and so forth. This aspect of Palestine's heritage industry is popular among Palestinians and can be found in many homes. In a sense, these objects enable people to furnish their modern day homes with a traditional feel and to display their national identity. Restaurants also decorate their interiors with embroidered objects, traditional pots and cooking utensils to create a traditional ambiance. The consumption and display of these objects works to redefine the peasant/

national identity particularly now that Palestine's economy is becoming more consumer orientated. What is interesting about the embroidery is the transformation it continually undergoes. One can view it as a living tradition which is not stagnant but rather evolves with time and changes in lifestyle. This is evident, I think, in its reproduction on household items. As household furnishings have expanded so have the spaces on which the embroidery appears, whereas in the past a peasant woman might have created a few cushions for her new home using traditional stitch work.

The transformations are also part of a change in the production of embroidery, and here we come to the question of gender roles once again. In the past a young girl would have been intiated into the language of the costume in terms of its patterns and stitches, their names and their functions at an early age. As she matured she would produce panels of embroidery for her wedding dress and trousseau.[18] The costumes were important for displaying her embroidery skills and her family's wealth, and the dresses celebrated her membership of the community through reproduction of the village's distinctive patterns.

Patterns evolved continually.[19] Women were inspired by the costumes of other villages and by new fabrics that entered the market and, by the 1930s, prosperous peasant women were sending their dresses to Bethlehem to have the chest panels embroidered there as the women of the town were famed for their couching stichwork.[20] Thus patterns of production were changing with the advent of modernity. The war of 1948 however completely disrupted the social relations which grounded the production and the meaning of the dresses. As land was lost, Palestinians were transformed into refugees and village structures and communities fragmented. The continuation and preservation of the tradition therefore dispersed into a number of different forms.

Preservation of the costume was taken up by people who began collecting them. Many of these collections were started by upper class women for whom charitable work of this kind did not conflict with the prestige of their class position (or what was seen as appropriate work for upper class women). At the same time such projects also enabled them to articulate their commitment to the national cause. Their focus on historic dresses, rather than contemporary costumes, can also be understood in terms of the issues of authenticity, for it is through the display of dresses and traditional jewellery in their homes, and the collecting of historical costumes, that the upper class not only display their patriotism but also their class position. Their interest is in the material culture of the peasantry of the past rather than the present.

Transformations in Palestinian society have also brought about a change in the patterns of production of embroidered items and dresses. While many women continue to create dresses for themselves and family members, embroidery has again become a way for women to earn money to support themselves and their families within the traditional boundaries of what is seen as women's work. For women such work does not conflict with their domestic responsibilities as it is often undertaken in their own homes. They will often sell their work on an individual basis, work for womens' organisations which have small shops for the sale of embroidered items, or supply merchants.

Expansion in the demand for embroidered items also has influenced a transformation in the patterns of embroidery. As embroidery is fitted to new objects, new patterns emerge that have become part and parcel of the evolvement of traditional embroidery. Significantly, both the collecting of costumes by upper class women and the work of embroidering by village and camp women also embodies the role of women as the 'preservers of cultural identity'. At the same time, embroidered items are bought as part of a display of national identity and as a way of supporting women's organisations and the embroiderers.

The Dress and Representations of Identity

I have written at length about the representation and reproduction of embroidery made by Palestinian peasant women in the past, but the peasant costume is also worn by many Palestinian women today, which makes it such an interesting heritage item.

The older generation of women from villages and refugees camps wear dresses with traditional embroidery as part of their everyday clothing. The dress in a sense is an intimate part of their identity, and women will have a considerable number of different dresses in their wardrobe. Some women may wear their dresses frequently, while others on special occasions, such as weddings, engagements and feast days – spaces for the reproduction of social memory. For the henna party before my wedding, at which the women of my husband's family came to present me with henna (traditionally used to adorn the bride's hands and feet), I chose to wear a contemporary version of the costume.

Women who wore the costume to this party came to the wedding in formal dresses and suits. The dresses have been created by the women themselves, by female family relatives or have been bought. Women will wear dresses whose stitch work comes from towns and villages which may not be their own place of origin. These dresses present the transformation and fluidity of traditions: particular cuts go in and out of fashion; the size and nature of waistbands change as do the shape of sleeves; patterns of stitch work are constantly evolving and so too are the threads and fabrics as synthetic materials enter the market.

During the Intifada, flag dresses emerged in which traditional patterns were replaced by patterns which incorporated the colours of the flag (which was banned at the time) and the map of the whole of Palestine. With these dresses, women were using the space of their bodies to represent their national identity explicitly. The embroidery patterns have also been adapted to modern day clothing: waistcoats, jackets, slippers, shawls and a range of accessories can be bought with traditional and more recent designs upon them.

At the beginning of this chapter I suggested that the dress provided a space for multiple identifications within the rubric of national identity and also a space for a multiplicity of imaginings about the peasantry. The representation of the woman in traditional costume became a metaphor for the motherland and its qualities and at the same time appropriated women's domestic work into the national discourse. Embroidery provides women with a livelihood while remaining within the framework of Palestinian society's idea of gender roles.

Flag Dresses from the Intifada Period

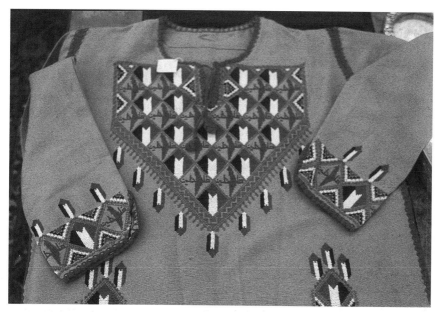

A blue Na'ani Dress. 1930s.
This dress is distinguished by its lavish embroidery and Bethlehem-style couching. This would have been worn by a young bride in the ceremony of going to the well and after the consummation of her marriage. (From the Widad Kawar Collection, Palestine).

Collecting the costume enables upper class women to display their commitment to the national cause while articulating their class position by distinguishing themselves from contemporary peasant women and their costumes. Embroidered home furnishings are used to create a link to the past, sustaining the central place of peasant identity as national identity. Women from villages and those who now live in refugee camps wear the dress in a elaborate expression of their identity which is a matrix of gender, social class and national identification.

In many ways then, embroidery and the costume can be read literally as the 'material' with which an idea of the motherland is developed and with which women articulate their national identity and create the fabric for the articulation of identity for the nation. It is a fabric which Palestinians continue to use to bind themselves to a lost homeland and to a peasant identity.

Notes

1. Bowman, *Tales of a Lost Land*, p. 32.
2. Nir, *Photographic Representations*, p. 186.
3. Waines, *The Failure of National Resistance*, p. 235.
4. Beinin, *Palestine and the Arab Israeli Conflict*, p. 102.
5. Khalidi, *All That Remains*, p. xxxi.
6. Weir, *Palestine Costume*, p. 107.
7. Tamari, *The Soul of the Nation*, p. 75.
8. Swedenberg, *The Peasant as National Signifier*, p. 24.
9. Hall, *Cultural Identity and Diaspora*, p. 224.
10. Daniels, *Fields of Vision*, p. 5.
11. Anderson, *Imagined Community*, p. 6.
12. Hunter, *A War by Other Means*, p. 80, Peretz *Intifada* pp. 55–57, and Warnock, *Land Before Honour*, p. 115.
13. Lentin, *(En)gendering Genocides*, p. 2, and Young, *The Politics of Healthcare*, p. 185–186.
14. Davis, Y, *Woman-Nation-State*, p. 92.
15. Aharoni & Mishal, *Speaking Stones*, p. 179.
16. Kandiyoti, *Identity and its Discontents*, p. 431.
17. Darwish, *Victims of a Map*, p. 21.
18. Weir, *Palestinian Costume*, p. 101.
19. Weir, Ibid. pp. 113–116.
20. Weir, Ibid. pp. 127–133.

Bibliography

Aharoni, *Reuben and Mishal*, Shaul, Speaking Stones: Communiqués from the Intifada (New York: Syracuse University Press, 1994).

Anderson, Benedict, *Imagined Communities; Reflections on the Origin and Spread of Nationalism* (London: Verso, 1991).

Beinin, Joel. 'Palestine and the Arab-Israeli Conflict for Beginners' in Beinin, J and Lockman, Z. (eds), *Intifada: The Palestinian Uprising Against Israeli Occupation* (London: I.B. Tauris, 1989).

Bowman, Glenn, 'Tales of The Lost Land; Palestinian Identity and the Formation of Nationalist Consciousness', in *New Formations*, No. 5.

Daniels, Stephen, *Fields of Vision: Landscape Imagery and National Identity in England and the United States* (Cambridge: Polity Press, 1993).

Darwish, Mahmoud & Al Qasim, Samih, *Victims of a Map* (London: Al Saqi Books, 1984).

Hall, Stuart, 'Cultural Identity and Diaspora' in J. Rutherford (ed), *Identity* (London: Lawrence and Wishart, 1990).

Hunter, F. Robert, *The Palestinian Uprising: A War by Other Means*, (London: I.B. Tauris, 1991).

Kandiyoti, Denis, 'Identity and its Discontents: Women and the Nation' in *Millennium: Journal of International Studies*, Vol. 20: No. 3, 1991.

Khalidi, Walid, *All That Remains; The Palestinian Villages Occupied and Depopulated by Israel* (Washington D.C: The Institute of Palestinian Studies, 1992).

Lentin, Ronit, '(En)gendering Genocides' in Lentin, R. (ed.), *Gender and Catastrophe* (London: Zed Books, 1997).

Nir, Yeshayahu, 'Photographic Representations and Social Interaction; The Case of The Holy Land' in *History of Photography*, Vol. 19: N. 3, 1995.

Peretz, Don, *Intifada: The Palestinian Uprising* (London: Westview Press, 1990).

Swedenberg, Ted, 'The Palestinian Peasant as National Signifier' in *Anthropological Quarterly*. Vol. 63: No.1. 1990.

Tamari, Selim, 'Soul of the Nation: The Fallah in the Eyes of the Urban Intelligentsia' in Bowman, G. (ed), *Review of Middle East Studies*, London, 1991.

Waines, David, 'Failure of the Nationalist Resistance' in Lughod, A.I. (ed), *The Transformation of Palestine; Essays on the Origins and Development of the Arab-Israeli Conflict*. (Evanston: Northwestern University Press, 1971).

Warnock, Kitty, *Land Before Honour: Palestinian Women in the Occupied Territories* (London: Macmillan Education Ltd., 1990).

Weir, Shelagh, *Palestinian Costume* (London: British Museum Press, 1994).

Young, G. Elise, 'A Feminist Politics of Healthcare: The case of Palestinian Women Under Israeli Occupation, 1979–1982' in Mayer, T. (ed), *Women and the Israeli Occupation; The Politics of Change* (London and New York: Routledge, 1994).

Yuval- Davis, Nira, 'National Reproduction and The Demographic Race in Israel' in Yuval-Davis & Anthias, F (eds), *Woman-Nation-State* (London: Macmillan, 1989).

KIM SOOJA'S BOTTARI AND HER JOURNEY

Sunjung Kim

Bottari is the traditional wrapping cloth of Korea. Bottari, or bundle, has had many uses. Traditionally made by women of all classes of society, they were used to cover food and store things, wrap clothing, move house, or for sending as gifts and other precious items. One translation of bottari is 'wrapping luggage with a wrapping cloth'. Such cloths may be embroidered, painted, made from oiled paper, patchwork or just plain cloth. The most popular wrapping cloths used patchwork designs and were made from small pieces of discarded scraps. Similar to the practice of quilting, these bottari were made by stitching patches of bright cloth onto the surface of a blanket. A simple sheet could be transformed into a colourful blanket and later used as a bed cover. Kim Sooja is a Korean artist who has deliberately chosen to work with the meanings and traditions of bottari made by ordinary people so as to create new works of art. As the artist related to me in my interview with her:

> As a medium, bottari is traditionally feminine. In Korean the expression to 'bundle up a bottari' means that a woman has lost her status in the household and has been forced out. Bottari also has significance as a container, or vessel, for carrying and transporting all sorts of goods. It can be unwrapped just as it can be bundled up and in this regard I see our body as being, in the subtlest kind of way, a kind of bottari.[1]

In this essay I will discuss some of the ways in which Kim Sooja has used bottari in her work and also touch on some feminist elements that are implicated in her practice. My discussion can be viewed within the context and transformations that have taken place in her work since the 1980s.

Korean women are taught from an early age to sew and develop needlework skills. Consequently, making wrapping cloths can never be separated from women's everyday life just as the blankets and bedclothes they make are indispensable objects in daily use. As such bottaris hold a special place for 'conveying buried memories and pain, as well as life's quiet passions'.[2] Blankets and bedclothes offer a place for rest when one is tired. As humans we are born on a blanket and die in one. Cloth protects and decorates: it is an essential element of life. The blanket is a site for human life and a place of its joy, anger, grief and pleasure. In Korea, traditional folk belief suggests that good luck and happiness can be preserved inside the cloth. The patterns on the blanket are ornaments and symbols that encompass our aspirations, such as fertility, health and longevity. The colours also have symbolic meaning.[3]

As I have already mentioned, Kim Sooja is an artist who visually and consciously combined tradition with contemporary art in an effective way. In my view, many contemporary artists have tried to offer new ways of working with conventional materials and concepts whilst still retaining their traditional distinctive character, but I think none have been as successful as Kim Sooja. In many works, women artists refer to the traditional labour associated with sewing and material. They introduce craft skills such as quilting and knitting into their work and these elements have often referred to their individual lives and memories. This approach has been associated with tendencies in feminist art, but I do not think I would define Kim Sooja simply as a feminist artist, although feminist traits can be found in her work.

The Works Prior to Bottari

Kim Sooja graduated from art college and graduate school in Korea in the 1970s. At that time, 'monochrome' was the dominant form of art along with other styles and experiments. During her studies, Kim was mainly influenced by formalism and conceptual art and, keeping these various trends of modern art in mind, her conceptual work was initially concerned with questions of 'the surface'. Although she experimented with various styles and expressions, she struggled to expand her vision and find her voice. In 1983, an incident occurred which had a new and lasting influence on her work. While sewing a blanket with her mother, Kim gained a new insight into cloth. She experienced a feeling of complete immersion in the realm of infinity. This experience led her to experiment with cloth and its surface, and resulted in a two-dimensional work which she has described as follows:

'In the midst of a common act of sewing blankets with my mother, I had a clandestine and surprising experience in which all of my senses, thoughts and activities all coincided with one another. In this experience, I discovered the possibility that so many memories, pains and affection of life buried unnoticed so far could be connoted in it. I was totally fascinated by the lines of longitude and latitude as the basic structure of cloth; its primordial colour; the feeling of identity between the cloth and me while it is being sewn; and the curious nostalgia evoked by those things.[4]

While sewing blankets, Kim found a new possibility of overcoming the limits of the two dimensional surface through the process of moving the needle above and beneath the cloth, and began to use this experience in her work. Such works were significant in that they connected women's everyday life to art work through the use of the material of cloth and the activity of sewing. Many Korean women artists use 'sewing' in their work, while others reference the human body. Kim Sooja's early works use sewing as representative of these early ideas about women's work and labour. More recently, she has consciously used the body:

'I regard botarri as the body itself. Like botarri, which can be bundled and unwrapped, the presence of the body lingers and departs. The cloth, in my view, is like our skin'.[5]

For me, her sewing works evoke a sense of femininity, labour and healing. However, there is also a difference between Kim Sooja's early work and many other feminist art forms since she uses fabric as canvas, which is a surface. In addition, she uses needlework as a tool, which asks endless questions on this border of surface trying to identify the subject and the object.

In the 1980s many Korean artists began to escape from the formalist, minimal monochrome art of the 1970s and related their works to social issues. They began to treat reality as a basis for a critical practice that represented social and political ideas. These practices presented a resistance to existing art activities and to the social system. The Minjoong Art movement was established by a number of Korean artists who shared these ideals.[6]

As a consequence many artists turned their backs on the individualistic works of the 1970s and began to deal with real life, to develop a critical vision about their society and its politics. One of the great influences of Minjoong Art was that it made people think about art in terms of communication. Kim Sooja's introduction of everyday life into her practice through sewing processes can be seen as a result of this influence. But she never joined the group since she did not agree with group activism and the fixed ideas, systems and power it holds over the individual. She continued to work on pieces in which canvas and painting were replaced by cloth and sewing. Such works can be described as modernist in that the work of sewing and cloth was done within the two dimensional surface.

The act of sewing necessarily accompanies the material of cloth. The action is repeated across the surface above and beneath. Kim attempted to overcome the limitations of the 'surface' through repetitive horizontal and vertical stitching. Paints were applied over the colours and patterns of the cloth with brush strokes, line drawings and stitched marks. These showed the variation of space. The action of sewing enabled the artist to interact with the material of cloth. In sewing, Kim engages with the surface simultaneously extending the space. I think that the introduction of cloth

Kim Sooja: **Portrait of Yourself** (1985)
used clothes, threads, acrylics, crayon, Chinese ink
190 x 277cm (75 x 109in)

and sewing into her art work brings the realm of the feminine into the art world and overcomes the exclusion of ideas and practices which were prevented by modernism in a Confucian society. Kim seeks to transcend gender difference and to celebrate the universal value of the human being.

Kim also produced collage works which used cloth and needle instead of canvas and paint. Although she added drawing or paint to the cloth in *Dans Ma Chambre* (1988), the cloth work still sticks to the square surface.

Since the early 1990s, Kim has wrapped her objects, using the title *Deductive Object*. In such works, Kim wrapped the cloth or hung it around common objects such as farming tools, sticks, ladders and laundry bars.

These works were significant in that Kim attempted to escape materiality and the frame imposed upon it by the painting. She still called these attempts 'deductive' because she wanted to get out of her earlier inductive works in which materials were assembled and connected by sewing. Deductive works reconfirm the structure of the object through the activity of wrapping it. As Kim has observed:

'With my objects it's as though I'm bandaging a wound. I wrap the object as if I was treating a wound, and through the wrapping

Kim Sooja: **Deductive Object** (1993)
used clothes wrapped with used bedcovers

and bandaging, the objects are transformed into something feminine'.[7]

The two dimensional frame of painting was left behind. A freer placement of shapes and objects on the wall was now possible. As the critic Oh Kwang Soo remarked:

'Even though there still remains the concept of her early paintings that are hung on the wall, most of Kim Sooja's works bear strong tendency toward three dimensionality. Although still wary of the wall, Kim's work is a world of painting turning its back on reality, out of the illusion and into the direct reality. Therefore, her works got out of the concept of painting or drawing and consisted of stitching, weaving or wrapping direct materials. In these works, Kim stresses the meaning of assemblage of things rather than just sewing them together, while her early works consisted of quilts'.[8]

This commentary suggests that Kim Sooja's work deals with the relationship between the cloth and the space in addition to revealing the cloth as cloth. Cloth has a number of purposes and meanings for people whether as blankets or as clothes. Other than a visible meaning, an invisible meaning also exists within the cloth. The ancestors of Korean people believed in transmigrations and the invisible spirit. For the ancestors, cloth is the best material to convey the spirit. I think that Kim evokes the immaterial through the materiality of cloth. Just as she had once experienced the feeling of unity with her mother through sewing together, Kim 'converses' with an invisible being through the medium of cloth.

In her P.S.1 studio residency in America (1992 and 1993), a series of works stretched the limits of merely experimenting with Korean material. This can be seen in one of the *Deductive Object* pieces made in 1993. Kim collected a large amount of cloth and transformed it into assemblages. These moved from the form of painting stuck inside the square frame to the three-dimensional form of the object and then into space.

Mind and the World illustrates this gradual development. In this oval shaped work, a pile of cloth was attached and stacked to the wall. Bamboo was connected to the pieces on the floor and on the wall. Different clothes were arranged in an oval shape and placed on the wall. Bamboos were wrapped with cloth as a supporting element. The use of bamboos reminds me of a needle form. In earlier works this needle form was only visible as the trace of a thread it left behind but in *Mind and the World*, the needle takes on multiple meanings. It connects the work and the earth, the artist's and the viewer's mind. The original function of a needle is to connect patches of cloth but Kim uses it as a vertical force in horizontal space. All the works she made previously seem to converge, thereby establishing themselves as a new force. In my view, *Mind and the World* is a work of total harmony as it brings together all elements: assemblage, sewing and winding, shape and colour.

Many *Deductive Objects* works were produced and contributed to new installation practice. In the one made for the 5th Istanbul Biennale, entitled *Deductive Object – dedicated to my marriage*, patches of crushed cloth were pushed into the cracks of the wall in her studio, creating an autobiographical message through the use of traditional Korean clothes or cloth. For the first time she completed a work by utilising the whole space of her studio. Both the form of placement and the relationship between art work and space was changed. America profoundly affected Kim's practice in several different ways. Firstly, she expanded the concept of space and secondly, bamboos stood in for the structural qualities and metaphoric possibilities of a needle form.

Bottari

The bottari reappeared, as Kim noted:

> 'The bottari has always been around us. The bottari was in my studio even before I worked on it. I just did not notice it. Then when I happened to turn my face accidentally in the P.S.1 studio, the bottari was there. I myself did not notice the patches of cloth wrapped in a bottari that I had intended to use for cloth work. That bottari was a totally new one. It was surely a sculpture and a painting'.[9]

Having abandoned the idea of placing cloth only within a frame, Kim wrapped a variety of objects, placing them on the floor and the wall. Although similar to the artist Christo in terms of the action of wrapping, Kim's wrapping work stresses the connection with everyday experience.

The bottari was defined as crossing the boundary between painting and sculpture. Kim's work was no longer a matter of form and composition but began to unfold in a different dimension, in much the same way as Marcel Duchamp could no longer be a futurist painter after inventing the ready-made painting. Bottari, however, is an ambiguous object that cannot be construed simply as a ready-made. Unlike the transformation of industrial products such as bicycle wheels or toilets into works of art as a result of the artist's choice, signature and exhibition, there is no boundary between the bottari as a work of art and as a common object.[10]

The Essence of Bottari

The common function of bottari is twofold. They are used for official functions and ceremonies and by ordinary people to store, wrap and carry things when on the move. Kim Sooja's bottari works embrace the activity of wrapping as a sign of being on the move as well as functioning as a 'real' bottari containing patches of cloth. The bottari in this context occupies an ambiguous position between life and art.

The bottari installed in a villa, contemporary gallery, museum or outside in the world takes on very different meanings (see colour plate 9).

The bottari is temporal in character. It is tied with bedclothes but inside there are used clothes. Clothes contain individual memories, stains and smells and the artist's experience, and exist as a part of the body. In human life, clothes have dual aspects of protection. They protect us from the cold and danger and signify the wearer's taste. The activity of wrapping up clothes into a bottari can be interpreted in many ways. To wrap up means protection and confinement at the same time. The confinement signifies severance from the outside world. To wrap up also signifies women's status in Korean society. As if wrapped up, Korean women are confined in the name of protection. The artist sees these blankets and bedclothes as places on which we are born and die, a foundational field which is the frame of our lives. To women, a blanket is a comfortable resting place during the night while being related to the bed in a sexual sense as well. Women give birth to children on a blanket. Thus it is a space where women continue human history. The blanket was also a symbol of oppression by Confucian morals and strict social ideology during the Chosun Dynasty (1392–1910). Within a social hierarchy that privileged men, women found pleasure and emotional survival through their needlework. Sewing was one of the few accepted activities that they could do. In a society in which the expression of colour was prohibited, Korean women used colour to decorate their blankets and bedclothes and communicate their hope. At a time when bright colours were not allowed in ordinary life, the blanket could be as brilliant in colour as women liked.

In her more recent work, Kim Sooja allows bedclothes and blankets to take on a meaning of 'invitation'. By spreading a blanket across a table in a public restaurant, Kim's work quietly sneaks into the ordinary life of people eating and talking outside the confines of a domestic interior. To place a bedcover on an eating table can be read as an attack on traditional custom. In Confucian society men and women eating together in public was strictly taboo. They lived in separate quarters and the kitchen was located within the women's area. In Kim's 'used bedcover' work, the blanket acts as a sign of resistance against this convention. In this respect, I think Kim Sooja is an example of an artist who questions convention and, by doing so, reveals the expressive power of an ordinary object such as bottari. I believe that Kim's life experience is accurately represented in bottari. The conservative Confucian tradition, which influenced her youth, finds expression in her work. In the shade of men, Korean women are like shadows without existence. Women are responsible for domestic economy and Kim's work evokes something for me about middle-aged women, (rather than women in general), and the renunciation of femininity. In other words, women appear as maternal beings who embrace and cure everything.

Now the bottari no longer stays in a gallery environment but is moved onto the top of a truck, into nature or becomes a shrine. In *A Laundry Field – Sewing into Walking, Looking into Sewing*, Kim hung bedcovers with laundry clips as if hanging real laundry. This bedcover installation occupied the whole space and could be viewed from various angles. The work was used as a stage ornament for a dance performance.[11]

Video Works

Bedcovers and bottari are used as signs of a metaphorical and literal journey in Kim Sooja's video works. In 1997, she travelled from Seoul through several other Korean cities before returning again to Seoul. The journey took eleven days and many bottari were loaded on the truck.

In *2727 kilometres Bottari Truck*, the meanings of 'migration' and 'origin' are extended as Kim travelled and 'performed' around the whole country. The video made en route was shown in *Cities on the Move*, an exhibition organised by Hans Ulrich Obrist and Hou Hanru. As I note from the title of the show, this whole curatorial project dealt with the topic of nomadism. *Cities on the Move – 2727kilometres Bottari Truck* encapsulates two themes: the artist's memory of her early days when she had to move constantly (her father was a military man), and her current experience of travelling all over the world for artistic projects. This is a journey of body and soul together and a journey into the memory and the past.

Kim Sooja: **Cities on the Move – 2727 kilometres Bottari Truck** (1997)
1 ton truck, used clothes wrapped with used bedcovers
an 11-day performance throughout Korea

Usually a journey is a movement between places, but Kim Sooja's journey shows the travel of time through the transition of places. The vertical concept of time is added to Kim's journey so that the journey in general becomes a linear movement between places. A similar work was made for the Venice Biennial in 1999.

Kim's bottari truck is both a symbol for her journey to other cities and other worlds, and a comment on those displaced from their homelands. She identifies the bottari with herself. She faces herself in the front mirror of the truck and confronts her past experiences. In all her video works, the identification with 'the journey into the other world' is constantly visualised.

In a video piece that records a performance in Delhi, Kim ended her identification with the bottari and made herself a needle sewing the earth, that is, *A Needle Woman*. This work shows how Kim identifies herself with the needle (see colour plate 10). She conceptualises the activity of sewing. While considering this activity as 'breathing or communication', she identifies walking and staring with sewing. *Mind and the World* was the first work in which this concept of sewing was stressed. In *Sewing into Walking,*

Kim herself is a needle, connecting the bedcovers on the ground with the earth. In her video works, Kim deploys used clothes, bottari and video monitors to connect the exhibition space and the viewers with the activity of sewing. The artist has said, 'previously thread and needle sewed cloth whereas this time my body is a medium that sews wide cloth that is nature'.

As we can see in this remark, Kim's needlework has evolved from the actual activity of sewing into conceptual sewing, revealing the relationship of intertwining without thread and needle. The artist sews the common life, environment and nature with her own body. This action replaces the needle. A needle can also be a tool that hurts, but it can be also be a tool that cures, as in Oriental medicine.

Kim is a needle that connects the body and the soul. Although the needle connects, it does not leave its trace. Kim herself becomes a needle to remove her own being. The responses of passers-by are diverse: the pedestrians in Tokyo look totally disinterested; the occasionally looking back Chinese in Shanghai appear to be curious; and the Indians stop and stare at the artist. The artist is a needle that continues to sew her with passers-by. In the repeated sewing the artist disappears and nothing remains.

In *Laundry Woman* made in India in 2000, Kim's empty state of mind appears more emphasized. In one scene, Kim meets the souls, as the remains of a burnt dead body passes by in front of the Yamuna. Kim's body is slowly assimilated into the river. She is free from all thoughts and ideas and goes into a different state of mind. As in all her video works, her activity is minimal. Many stories are condensed as her works change from the bottari to the needle and then to nature. Kim once sewed the world with her body as medium but now she tells us another story with her eye and mind. As Rosalind Krauss has observed, the real medium of video art is not the mechanical apparatus but the psychical circumstance. In Kim's video work one can feel the state of being nothing and experience the correspondence with nature without any skill.[12]

In conclusion I believe that Kim positions her itinerary between life and death. She sees each sewing stitch as an endless itinerary. She is the needle that travels across the cloth. She once discovered this while sewing blankets with her mother, and then overcame the limitation of the two-dimensional surface by sewing onto a blanket. In a progressive variation of bottari works, Kim developed the concept of journey or migration into *2727 kilometres Bottari Truck*, then she evolved into *Needle Woman*, and finally in her video works the needle is identified with the body. The thread has continuity and circularity. This aspect of continuity and circularity of life is apparent in her work. This also signifies transmigration in Buddhism.

Kim Sooja's journey is not over yet.

Notes

1. Kim Sun-Jung, *Interview with Four Korean Women Artists*, Art Asia-Pacific Vol. 3, 1996, p. 59.
2. Ibid. p. 60.
3. For further analysis on this subject, see Huh Dong-hwa's essay, 'History and art in traditional wrapping cloths', in Claire Roberts and Huh Dong-hwa (eds), *Rapt in Colour: Korean textiles and costumes of the Chosen Dynasty* (Sydney: Powerhouse Museum and The National Museum of Korean Embroidery, 1998) p. 21. I think it useful to quote one extract here as it impacts on how Kim Sooja uses the meanings of bottari in her work; 'the warm colours represent the sun and blood, while blues and greens suggest the trees, grass, birth, growth and prosperity. These five colours correspond to the four points of the compass and the centre; the five elements of the weather (cold, warmth, wind, dryness and humidity); the five elements of the universe (wood, fire, metal, water and earth); the four seasonal differences (spring, summer, autumn and winter); and the five blessings (longevity, wealth, success, health and luck)'.
4. Taken from the artist's statement, Exhibition Catalogue, Gallery Hyundai, Seoul, 1988.
5. Ibid. p. 58.
6. Minjoong Art is a radical form of art fostered by the political upheaval during the 1980s. After the Kwangju Democratization Movement, many forms of social movement emerged and spread across the whole country. Naturally they had a strong impact on the new direction of art. Artists started to stand for anti-modernism and incorporated a new reflection of reality into their art. They also advocated direct comments and criticism of social events, and embraced group activities such as issuing manifestos and other publications.
7. Ibid. p. 60.
8. Oh Kwang Soo, A *Return to the Archetype: Recent Works of Soo Ja Kim*, essay for exhibition catalogue, Gallery Hyundai, Seoul, 1991.
9. Taken from the artist's statement, Exhibition Catalogue, Gallery Hyundai, 1988.
10. Kim Ai-Ryung, 'Sooja Kim, the Wrapping View of Art and Life', *Wolgan Misool,* October 1999, pp. 162–171.
11. Exhibition Catalogue, Video Installation by Kim Sooja: *A Needle Woman*, 2000, ICC, Japan.
12. Ibid.

NORDIC TEXTILE TRADITIONS AND VISIONS: A BASIS FOR RECONSIDERATION

Lisbeth Tolstrup

In this essay I draw on over 20 years of experience as a textile designer and critic in order to analyse the Nordic textile art scene from a historical perspective. Additionally, contemporary debates which surround the Nordic Triennial of Textiles during the period 1976–96 inform the ways in which textile art has been interpreted within Denmark, Norway, Sweden, Finland and Iceland.

From my perspective, textile art is once again in the middle of a struggle for identity and respect. Students, lecturers, art critics and curators are looking for ways to articulate and relate to other visual and material practices. If textile art has been problematically viewed as the younger sister of craft and the outsider of aesthetic theory, I would argue that there have been many attempts to define it during the last 50 years and on its own terms. These attempts have included the search for the definition of a textile identity. It has often seemed to me like a never-ending contradiction. As soon as textile art develops in related areas, such as design, applied art, fashion or craft, then its significance in relation to the conventions of fine art is minimalised. The question is, if it matters at all. Is there any reason to relate the field of textiles in the sense of art-based classification, rather than to relate the works of those artists who consider themselves part of a textile art curriculum? It seems so simple, for someone involved professionally to identify, classify and criticise, but seen from an outside point of view, it is almost impossible to find well articulated sources that go beyond pure description, historical relativeness or open attempts to relate to the actual art scene. And that is in spite of the fact that the history of modern textiles follows at least three directions (maybe four, if the interrelations between textile art and feminism count as one).[1]

The conventional ways in which textiles are classified on the Nordic scene involve home craft, handicraft, commissions and reproduction, hand based as well as industrially manufactured. This involves a well-known method of description, developed as a museal tool and referred to as a purely object-focused way of analysing things. There has not been much space for a more critical, a more art-related or even a more experimental approach. It might seem conventional to separate it like this, but nevertheless this is the way it is done among politicians, curators and art critics. I think that there have been some attempts to change the form, considered to be 'the form' used by art historians and ethnographers. And it has its guardians! Charlotte Paludan of The Danish Museum of Decorative Art recently criticised a book about the Danish weaver and textile designer Vibeke Klint, written by another weaver Inge Alifrangis. Paludan based her criticism on the fact that Alifrangis is too closely related to Klint, being a former student and colleague, and therefore not capable of standing at a critical distance.

I find that the criticism, however relevant it might be from a curator's point of view, demonstrates the difference between a conventionally rooted way of writing scientifically and a more experienced-based and personal way of writing. Whilst these methods are well established within the traditions of ethnographical and art historical research, direct contact with contemporary textile art and its makers permits experimental ways of writing criticism. However, I used to think that the right way to work and write was to define textile art on its own terms and conditions but I am not so convinced now, if that means isolation from the rest of the art scene. There is another strong convention of writing that has affected writing about textile art and which I think worth noting. The tradition of biography within fine art has been developed since the middle of the 18th century, while for textile artists it has depended on self-defining writing developed only over the last 40 years.

Juried exhibitions are also part of the contested field of representation and interpretation. For example, they have never been open for textile art, as they have for painting, sculptural work, graphics, and at times photo and art pieces of craft.[2] Since the 1920s and even earlier, textile artists themselves have tried to form workshops and later studios and groups to initiate exhibitions on their own terms, developing their own criteria for participation. Again this caused debate and dispute outside the very narrow textile field, especially for those artists who where not interested in classification, but only in the possibility of exhibiting in so-called better places.

If they succeeded in showing work in institutions of high repute in the arts, they seldom received much attention, because only a very few curators or art critics possessed the knowledge and vocabulary to inform an audience or produce interesting textile art criticism. It is common to see a review where design, the production of piece goods or tapestry are mixed up in one big confusion under the name of textile art. Again this raises the question of where we can locate the practices of textile art in visual and material culture. The discussion is as old as the new wave of textile art dating back to the 1960s. But it is still relevant, and since textile artists themselves often raise it because it is considered to be one of the barriers against the acceptance of textile art among other artists, curators and collectors.

Nordic Transitions

From this rather practical way of seeing things, I am trying to find a few examples of how description and classification can interrelate on a Nordic basis.[3] One of the best examples is to be found in the book *Svenska Textilier 1890–1990*, which is an attempt to give a broad overview of the history and textiles of one country seen from seven different points of view.[4] The book is divided into eight main chapters covering history, important associations, commissions and politically related textiles, just to name some of them. The shorter chapter contains ten biographies of individuals whom the authors consider important for the period. The result is a book based on knowledge and research (unfortunately only in Swedish) but with a good introduction to textiles as a traditional field of home craft, industrial production and commissioning for churches and industry.

For me, one of the most interesting in this sense is a chapter by Jan Brunius, in which he tries to place Swedish textile art in the context of the art scene of the 1960s.[5] I do not think he ever really gets into it however, even though he refers to women's liberation and feminist thinking (which was strong in Sweden), along with a growing consciousness of the environment and solidarity with working class politics. One reason might be that the Handicraft Society (Handarbetets Vänner) in those years offered a wide range of workshop services including tapestry weaving and embroidery. It meant that there was a basis for commissions (read: earning money) and at the same time something to revolt against. Another reason might be that Brunius never really found any interest himself or amongst his readers for including an analysis of textile art as part of the avant-garde international art scene, even though it was developing during the period he was writing his book.

A deeper conflict is probably to be found in the different values that characterised the bourgeois, the workshops and the changes within the educational field in the 1960s and 1970s. An interesting point is that some of the leading figures in the Swedish textile field were to be found both in the workshop and in the educational field: that it was possible for them on the one hand to carry out a classical, Nordic based but French influenced tapestry production, and on the other, to be open to international movements within textile art during the 1960s. This example from Sweden can be found elsewhere in Nordic countries particularly when books evoke a similar paradox, namely a convention for seeing 'pure' production of tapestries, lace or linen as a natural part of tradition, while expressive textiles are considered new and unique, as long as the artists call themselves artists and not craftspeople.

In the Nordic countries textiles are based on a construction (or literally speaking a grid) that involves tradition, history and international influence. The modern history of textiles is not old, but it is strong if it is related to the industrial era and this may be the real obstacle to developing an expressive art form based on textiles. There is no reason here to repeat the well-known discussion about whether textiles as an art form should be based on technical, materialistic or expressive means; it seems more relevant to discuss a basis for using the term 'art' in relation to textiles in a Nordic context.

The Nordic Triennial of Textiles

The idea of a Nordic Triennial of Textiles originated in Denmark and was initiated in 1974 by a small group of Danish artists from different positions in the textile field. It was close to the heart of these artists, who knew each other well and had good connections with artists in other Nordic countries. The inspiration of the Lausanne Biennial is obvious, though only a limited number of Nordic textile artists at that time had participated.[6] Or it might have been the strong influence of Nordic home craft which, for over 100 years, had been organised with its own rules and regulations on the exhibition of textiles. This I think was more a question of product presentation than an aesthetic viewpoint. And finally the close and well-defined relations between textile artists, architects and designers was influenced by the international functionalistic movement and defined by commissions. In conclusion, the Nordic Triennial was an attempt to make a new forum for artists in the field, a new platform for experiments, and as seen from a certain point of view, to reach a new audience which had never before considered textiles as a medium for artistic expression.

The project began in 1974 and the first Triennial was held in 1976. Five working groups and a jury consisting of five members were set up. The jury was made up of one representative from each Nordic country plus one other member. All work was collected in one place for selection. I think the result was a kaleidoscopic exhibition, more a reflection of the breadth of the field from a curatorial standpoint. The curators had problems with the wide range of work and the artists were inexperienced in dealing with the questions this presented. The work involved had proved overwhelming for both working groups and jury and it was decided that the next exhibition, planned to take place in 1979, should be juried within each country.

When the second Triennial was hung it was obvious that this new approach had failed. From a conscious attempt to define a field of expression, it had become a catalogue of Nordic textile tradition. This was interesting for those who understood what to look for, but represented (in my view) three steps back for those who had fought for textiles as a means of creative expression and were trying to reach for so-called international status.

The third Triennial (1982–3) and the fourth (1985–6) were juried as a whole but still under the auspices of the artists themselves. In the third Triennial, huge textile art works were hung, and revealed a tendency towards commission scale, while the fourth was the most internationally influenced. Textile artists had overcome their fear of two dominant influences: firstly that of French speaking Switzerland and secondly that of Eastern Europe. Certainly influence from Eastern Europe had been strong in earlier Triennials but now many textile art works indicated how much had been absorbed from Japan post the mid-1980s. This influence was similar to the one absorbed 100 years earlier following the opening of the Japanese borders and the big international exhibitions in the 1880s. It seemed obvious to me that many artists had visited the major exhibitions in Lausanne, Japan and the USA, and had seen that the size of individual pieces created an opportunity to reach new ways of working. Consequently, the Nordic Triennials became more diverse and more individual and showed a closer dialogue between the different textile scenes within Nordic countries.

The first ten years were one long struggle of fundraising. The five committees were exhausted by this task and were happy to accept an offer from The Nordic Arts Center in Helsinki to house the Triennial. The price they paid, however, was to allow curators to participate in the work of the jury. It was still a juried exhibition in 1989 (the fifth) and in 1992 (the sixth), while the seventh was invited and based on suggestions from three

- well received by artists, particularly those who had been involved in the
original idea and organisation of the Triennial.

The seventh was the last. I think the work in this final exhibition was of
a high standard but it seemed like the Triennial had lost its magic and
appeal. The balance between experiment and knowledge, and international
curiosity and local tradition, had disappeared in the attempt to make the
Triennial look like any other internationally acceptable exhibition within
the textile art field within a fine art context.[7]

Crisis for Experiments

The end of the Nordic Triennial meant, among other things, that there
was no longer a possibility of interrelating one's work across borders or in
larger museums and galleries. The inter-Nordic platform had vanished and
the struggle for acceptance from galleries, museums and critics had only
succeeded in a limited way. However, seen positively it also meant that
there had been a vision, and that many artists had dared to define themselves
as artists. I believe that one of the strongest impacts, and one which has not
received much attention, was on education for which the Triennial was a
rich source of inspiration for teachers and students alike. Textiles were now
seen as an expressive media, and working with them as a way of reinventing
a unique tradition as well as refreshing industrial design.

What was distinctive about the Triennial era was that it allowed for the
possibility of working in different spheres. Artists travelled outside their
national cultural and geographic boundaries and, in so doing, met other
artists and found their position on the national art scene. When Grete Balle
(Danish, born 1926) began her work, it was as a painter. It was not until
later that she took up weaving, inspired by an exhibition of Finnish 'ryas'
in Copenhagen. But that was only the beginning. Later she went to Poland,
where she visited the workshop of Maria Lasckiewicz (one of Magdalena
Abakanowicz's formative teachers). Both she and her husband, the painter
Mogens Balle, were members and participated in experiments with the
poet of Cobra, Christian Dotremont.[8] I have chosen Grete Balle as an
example of how diversely a textile artist can explore the fundamental basis
for her work, and how important it is to relate to different sources of the
field itself and at the same time be active in an artistic environment. She
did not, in my view, relate to a narrow textiles scene but preferred to work
very much on her own terms, sometimes focusing on textiles, sometimes
on painting and sometimes on graphic work.

There are others – Frida Hansen (Norwegian, 1855–1931), Hannah Ryggen (Norwegian, 1894–1970)[9] and Marie Gudme Leth (Danish, 1896–1997)[10] – just to mention a few – who wrote the textile history of the North. The story of Frida Hansen was unknown until the late 1970s, when the Norwegian art historian Anniken Thue published her research on the artist and curated an exhibition of some of her work. It is the story of a self taught woman who had to build a new life after a decline in her family fortune brought about by the 1880s depression. She developed a new method of transparent weaving which she patented in 1897. At the same time she distanced herself from traditional Norwegian weaving as practiced by the Homecraft Society, and traditional ways of working to commission. Her business thrived and some of her weavers went on to work in the art nouveau style which she herself had picked up and developed.

I think the main characteristic which unites Frida Hansen and Grete Balle is that they both explored their skill base and developed the medium's expressive potential despite being nearly a century apart. For me they are both modern examples of how to pioneer a field of artistic expression.

Grete Balle: **Drifting towards Green** (1992)
mixed media
2.5 x 4m (8 x 13ft)

The Conceptual and the Picturesque

Hundreds of pieces of work were on show over the seven Nordic Triennials. Among those who moved the boundaries of how work in the Triennials may be viewed was Ragna Robertsdottir (Iceland, born 1945), whose work references the textile movement of the 1980s and at the same time reflects the nature of Iceland and the minimalist and conceptual movement of the international art scene. Her first work was woven in strings of rope and later she used turf, rubber and lava. She used the whole room as a frame and managed to keep a strong sense of the textile, even when a piece was geometrically constructed with hundreds of lava stones. I think she was concise and precise in her expression and for me she represents one of the boundary movers.

In contrast to Ragna Robertsdottir, Elsa Agelii (Swedish, born 1938) used embroidery as her media, initially pursuing a narrative direction in her work, but in later pieces a more poetic, though critical attitude can be evidenced. While Robertsdottir was concrete and conceptual, Agelii referenced handicraft tradition, although she was breaking it at the same time by constructing her own images instead of patterns. She cited statements and poetry instead of repetitive ornaments and she chose, I think, an appropriate scale for her narratives to succeed (see colour plate 12).

As I mentioned earlier, there was little interest in the mid-1970s in exploring or even approaching classical tapestry weaving in Nordic countries. A few weavers were developing their own techniques, like Grete Balle, and others with her, but the mid-European tradition was not being taught or developed in general. A few weavers kept working, among whom Jenny Hansen (Danish, born 1951) has to be mentioned as an example of an artist who not only continues to dye her own yarns before weaving them, but also combines the picturesque possibilities of the computer with her skills on the loom. I think her intentions have moved from monochromatic fantasies to more and more colourful and detailed images. She sees this as a result of her sketching work on the computer, which offers her a wide range of ideas before the final one becomes a cartoon for the huge weavings (see colour plate 15).

These four artists can be seen both as representatives of different approaches to textile expression before, during and after the era of the Nordic Triennial, and as icons for the historical line based on homecraft, early design, production or even the basis for design – the movement-related line being the Biennials of Lausanne, the Triennials of Lodz, the competitions in Kyoto or the increasing interest in the Betonac exhibition held in Belgium, the Flexible exhibition in the Netherlands and the steady search for new platforms to compete on. The last line to be mentioned involves the early Dadaist movement, and later on Arte Povera, Fluxus and the stronger conceptual thinking of Joseph Beuys, Robert Morris and Meret Oppenheim who were working on the same borders of craft and art as many textile artists are today.

The struggle for identity, artistic as well as textile-related, is an ongoing process. Different classifications can and will be made in the light of increasing historical and theoretical interest, but they will always serve as tools for the living artist, as she/he strives to find their way in the actual context. New biennials or triennials will occur, new structures will form patterns, some will raise professional interest while others will just remain a wave in the sea of curiosity, highlighted by a moment of global interest, and disappearing with the next tide.

Notes

1. The three relations mentioned here are the historical, the movement-related and the conceptually-related aspect.
2. In Danish the expression 'Kunsthaandvaerk' (which is a combination of the words art and craft) is used. I have chosen to use the expression 'art pieces of craft'. It relates to the idea of well crafted objects made for the common purpose in opposition to pure decoration. The juried exhibition has a long tradition in Denmark. There are five which open up membership of professional associations and galleries.
3. 'Nordic' in general relates to the Nordic countries, considered to be Denmark, Norway, Sweden, Finland, Iceland, Faroe Islands and Greenland. Though in praxis, Greenland was never really active in the textile movement, one reason being that there was no art school there until the late 1990s and that textiles were considered to be home craft. The number of artists and craftspeople in the Faroe Islands was limited and they often went to Norway, Denmark and Sweden for their education.
4. Brunius, Jan; Danielson, Sofia; Ericsson, Anna-Marie; Hammar, Britta; Hovstadius, Barbro; Ridderstedt, Margareta; and Stensman, Mailis: *Svenska Textilier* (*Swedish Textiles*) *1890–1990*, Signum, Lund 1994.
5. *Svenska Textilier*, Ibid pp. 264–291.
6. The Biennial of Lausanne refers to La Biennale Internationale de la Tapisserie Ancienne et Moderne, which took place from 1962 to1995. It was initiated by the French tapestry weaver Jean Lurçat and his friend the gallery owner Pierre Paulli from Lausanne in Switzerland.
7. For further information on The Nordic Triennial of Textiles, it is still possible to get some of the catalogues for the 2nd–6th triennial, texted in Scandinavian languages as well as in English, by contacting the Danish weaver Nanna Hertoft, Kulsviervaenget 28, DK-2800 Lyngby. Nordisk Konstcentrum in Helsinki 1995 published the 7th catalogue (ISBN: 951–8955–49–2).
8. The name COBRA relates to the name of an artist group, named after three cities, Copenhagen, Brussels and Amsterdam, from which the founding members originated,

and among whom the Danish painter Asger Jorn might be the best known. Cobra was established in 1948 and was active as a group for only three years, but their ideas about the picture as a medium for culture, history and experiments went on and was explored by the individual artists.

9.   Hannah Ryggen is often identified as the mother of modern Norwegian tapestry. She was born in Malmo, Sweden in 1894, and trained as a teacher. She wanted to be a painter and took lessons from a Danish painter. This led to the dream of travelling as for so many other Nordic female artists of the time. In 1922 in Germany she met and married a young Norwegian artist called Hans Ryggen, They moved to Norway and soon after she began to weave, when she declared it was necessary for her to be an artist herself. She refused to work as a weaver for other artists, she never used sketches and wanted to express herself through the weaving. She was very interested in art and politics and often related her motifs to real life.

10.   Marie Gudme Leth was the first textile artist to work seriously with textile printing in Denmark. Educated in Germany, she subsequently developed her own techniques and patterns, and was the first textile artist to teach the printing class in the School of Applied Art in Copenhagen (from 1932).

BIBLIOGRAPHY

Adams, Clive, 'Wrapping the bundle', *Contemporary Art*, Spring 1996.

Aharoni, Reuben and Mishal, Shaul, Speaking Stones: Communiques from the Intifada (*New York: Syracuse University Press, 1994*).

Ahn Soyeon, '*Bottari* – The 1999 Venice Biennale', *Korea Pictorial*: Spring 1999.

Alifrangis, Inge, *Det danske aegte taeppe/Danish Handmade Rugs and Carpets* (Copenhagen: Rhodos, 1996).

Alifrangis, Inge, *Vaeveren Vibeke Klint/The Weaver Vibeke Klint* (Copenhagen: Rhodos, 1997).

Amelia, *Body Art: Performing the Subject* (Minneapolis: University of Minnesota Press, 1998).

Anderson, Benedict, *Imagined Communities; Reflections on the Origin and Spread of Nationalism* (London: Verso, 1991).

Askari, N. and Arthur, L., *Uncut Cloth Saris, Shawls and Sashes* (London: Merrell Holberton, 1999).

Bachelard, Gaston, *La Poétique de l'espace* (ed. Presses Universitaires de France, 1984 c. 1957).

Bahk Young Taik, 'Soo Ja Kim – To approach from Plane to three Dimension, a Bundle', *Space Journal: Interview*, June 1996.

Bal, Mieke, 'Telling Objects: A Narrative Perspective on Collecting' in John Elsner and Roger Cardinal (eds), *The Cultures of Collecting* (London: Reaktion Books Ltd, 1994).

Bataille, Georges, *Visions of Excess: Selected Writings 1927–1939* (Minneapolis: University of Minnesota Press, 1985).

Baudrillard, Jean, 'The Precession of Simulacra', in Brian Wallace (ed), *Art After Modernism*, The New Museum of Contemporary Art, New York in association with David R. Godine (Boston, 1984).

Beinin, Joel. 'Palestine and the Arab-Israeli Conflict for Beginners' in Beinin, J. and Lockman, Z. (eds), *Intifada: The Palestinian Uprising Against Israeli Occupation* (London: I.B. Tauris, 1989).

Benjamin, Jessica, *The Bonds of Love, Psychoanalysis, Feminism, and the Problem of Domination* (New York: Pantheon, 1988).

Benjamin, Walter, 'Unpacking My Library', in Hannah Arendt (ed), *Illuminations* (New York: Harcourt, Brace, Jovanovich, 1968).

Bonami, Francesco, 'Beyond The Borders, Our Borders'. *Flash Art International*, Nov-Dec 1995.

Bordo, Susan, 'The Body and the Reproduction of Femininity', in Jagger, Alison and Bordo, Susan (eds), *Gender, Body Knowledge* (Rutgers University Press, 1989).

Bowen, Stella, *Drawn from Life, A Memoir* (Sydney: Picador, 1999).

Bowman, Glenn, 'Tales of The Lost Land; Palestinian Identity and the Formation of Nationalist Consciousness', in *New Formations*, No.5.

Braidotti, Rosi, *Nomadic Subjects: Embodiment and Sexual Difference in Contemporary Feminist Theory* (New York: Columbia University Press, 1994).

Brunius, Jan; Danielson, Sofia; Ericsson, Anna-Marie; Hammar, Britta; Hovstadius, Barbro; Ridderstedt, Margareta, and Stensman, Mailis (eds), *Svenska Textilier/Swedish Textiles 1890–1990* (Signum: Lund, 1994).

Burman, Barbara (ed), *The Culture of Sewing: Gender, Consumption and Home Dressmaking* (Oxford UK and New York: Berg, 1999).

Calderon, Soel Rodas, 'Maya Textiles: Visions of Identity', http://alcor.concordia.ca/~textiles, 1997.

Catalogues: The Nordic Triennial of Textiles. No. 2–6: Nanna Hertoft, Kulsviervaenget 28, DK-2800 Lyngby, Denmark; No. 7: Nordisk Kunstcentrum, Helsinki 1995, SF

Coomaraswamy, A.K., *Art and Swadeshi* (New Delhi: Munshiram Manoharlal 1994).

Cooper, J.C., *Dictionary of Symbolic and Mythological Animals* (London: Harper Collins, 1992).

Corrin, Lisa G., *Mining the Museum* (Baltimore: The Contemporary, in co-operation with The New Press, New York, 1994).

Coxall, Helen, 'Re-presenting Marginalized Groups in Museums: The computer's 'second nature'?' in The Cutting Edge, Women's Research Group (eds) *Desire by Design: Bodies, Territories and New Technologies* (I.B. Tauris & Co. Ltd., 1999).

Daniels, Stephen, *Fields of Vision: Landscape Imagery and National Identity in England and the United States* (Cambridge: Polity Press, 1993).

Darwish, Mahmoud and Al Qasim, Samih, *Victims of a Map* (London: Al Saqi Books, 1984).

Deleuze, Gilles and Guattari, Felix, *Anti-Oedipus: Capitalism and Schizophrenia* (Minneapolis: University of Minnesota Press, 1992).

Douglas, Mary, *Purity and Danger: An Analysis of Concepts of Pollution and Taboo* (New York: Frederick A. Praeger, Publishers, 1966).

Ehrlich, Eugene, *Amo, Amas, Amat and More* (New York: Harper and Row, 1985).

Entwistle, Joanne and Wilson, Elizabeth, 'The Body Clothed', in *Addressing the Century – 100 Years of Art and Fashion* (London: Hayward Gallery Publishing, 1999).

Ferris, Alison, *Discursive Dress* (Wisconsin: John Michael Kohler Arts Center, 1994).

Fleming, Marnie, Soo-Ja Kim: *A Laundry Field-Sewing into Walking, Looking into Sewing* (Ontario: Oakville Galleries, 1997).

Gallagher, Winifred, *Working on God* (Random House: New York, 1999).

Gallop, Jane, 'The Body Politic', *Thinking Through the Body* (New York: Columbia University Press, 1988).

Garrett, Valery M., *A Collector's Guide to Chinese Dress Accessories* (Times Edition: Singapore, 1997).

Garrett, Valery M., *Chinese Clothing: An Illustrated Guide* (Hong Kong: Oxford University Press, 1999).

Gatens, Moira, *Imaginary Bodies, Ethics, Power and Corporeality* (London and New York: Routledge, 1996).

Giese, Diana, Astronauts, *Lost Souls & Dragons – Voices of today's Chinese Australians in conversation with Diana Giese* (St Lucia, Queensland: University of Queensland Press, 1997).

Gilbert, Helen; Khoo, Tseen and Lo, Jacqueline (eds), *Diaspora: Negotiating Asian-Australia* (St. Lucia, Queensland: Queensland University Press, 2000).

Gilroy, Paul, *The Black Atlantic Modernity and Double Consciousness* (London and New York: Verso, 1993).

Grosz, Elizabeth, *Volatile Bodies, Toward A Corporeal Feminism* (Bloomington and Indianapolis: Indiana University Press, 1994).

Grosz, Elizabeth, *Volatile Bodies: Toward a Corporeal Feminism* (Australia: Allen & Unwin, 1994).

Grynsztejn, Madeleline, 'CI: 99/00', *Carnegie International 1999/2000* (Pittsburgh: Carnegie Museum of Art, Carnegie Institute, 1999).

Hall, Stuart, 'Cultural Identity and Diaspora' in J. Rutherford (ed), *Identity* (London: Lawrence and Wishart, 1990).

Hanson, Karen, 'Dressing Down Dressing Up: The Philosophic Fear of Fashion', in Hem (ed), *Aesthetics in Feminist Perspective* (Bloomington and Indianapolis: Indiana University Press, 1993).

Heartney, Eleanor, 'Report from Istanbul – In the Realm of the Senses', *Art in America*, April 1998.

Hendrickson, Carol, *Weaving Identities: Construction of Dress and Self in a Highland Guatemala Town* (Texas: University of Texas Press, 1995).

Hornik, Susan, 'PACIFIC RIM: South KOREA', *Art News*, Summer, 1992.

Hunter, F. Robert, *The Palestinian Uprising: A War by Other Means* (London: I.B. Tauris, 1991).

Hwang In, 'Sewing into Walking-Cloth, Video, Sound Installation by Soo Ja Kim', *Space Journal*, January 1995.

Irigaray, Luce, *This Sex which Is Not One*, trans. Catherine Porter (Ithaca: Cornell University Press, 1985).

Jefferies, Janis and Layne, Barbara, 'Hacking the Museum: Electronic Textiles', John Gange (ed) in *ACT 4: Art Technology, Technique* (London: Pluto Press, 1997).

Jefferies, Janis, 'Text and Textiles: Weaving Across the Borderlines,' in Katy Deepwell (ed), *New Feminist Art Criticism: Critical Strategies* (New York: St. Martins Press, 1995).

Johnson, Alexandra, *The Hidden Writer: Diaries and the Creative Life* (New York: Anchor, 1997).

Jones, Glynis, 'Outrageous! Costume & Confections' in *Absolutely Mardi Gras – Costume and Design of the Sydney Gay & Lesbian Mardi Gras* (Sydney: Powerhouse Publishing and Doubleday, 1997).

Kandiyoti, Denis, 'Identity and its Discontents: Women and the Nation' in *Millennium: Journal of International Studies*, Vol. 20: No. 3, 1991.

Kang Sung Weon, 'Soo Ja Kim – An Individual Truth: The Language of Installation Work, Identity and Culture', *Space Journal*, June 1996.

Kaplan, Caren, *Questions of Travel: Postmodern Discourses on Displacement* (Duke University Press, 1998).

Kaplan, J. Louise, *Female Perversions* (London: Penguin Books 1991).

Kee, Joan, 'The Image Significant: Identity in Contemporary Korean Video Art', *Afterimage* Vol. 27 no.1, 1998.

Khalidi, Walid, *All That Remains; The Palestinian Villages Occupied and Depopulated by Israel* (Washington DC: The Institute of Palestinian Studies, 1992).

Kim Ai-Ryung, 'Soo Ja Kim – A Wrapping View of Art and Life', *Wolgan Misool*, October, 1999.

Kim Soo Ja, *Cloth and Life*, an artist's statement for the 5th Istanbul Biennale catalogue, 1997.

Kim Sun-Jung, 'Interview with four Korean Women Artists', *Art Asia-Pacific*, Vol. 3, 1996.

Kim Young-Ho, 'Bottari Project by Kim Soo-Ja', in *Roteiros* (24th Sao Paulo Biennale: 1998).

Kirschenblatt-Gimblett, Barbara, 'Confusing Pleasures', in Barbara Kirschenblatt-Gimblett (ed), *Destination Culture* (Berkeley: University of California Press, 1998).

Kuryluk, Ewa, *Veronica and Her Cloth: History, Symbolism, and Structure of a 'True' Image* (Cambridge, Massachusetts: Basil Blackwell Inc. 1991).

Laplanche, J. and Pontalis, J.B. *The Language of Psycho-Analysis* (New York: W. W. Norton & Company, 1973).

Lentin, Ronit, '(En)gendering Genocides' in Lentin, R. (ed.), *Gender and Catastrophe* (London: Zed Books, 1997).

Levin, Kim, 'Report from Seoul', *Sculpture* magazine, Nov-Dec 1992.

Lynton, Linda, *The Sari Styles: Patterns History Techniques* (London: Thames and Hudson, 1995).

Mackinnon, Alison, *Love and Freedom* (Cambridge: Cambridge University Press, U.K. 1997).

Martinez, Rosa, 'Istanbul Biennale', *Flash Art*, Nov–Dec 1998.

Menchú, Rigoberta, *I, Rigoberta Menchú*, Elisabeth Burrgos-Debray (ed) (London & New York: Verso, 1984).

Menon, Ritu and Bhasin, Kamla, *Borders & Boundaries Women in India's Partition* (New Brunswick, New Jersey: Rutgers University Press, 1998).

Modjeska, Drusilla, *Stravinsky's Lunch* (Sydney, Australia: Pan Macmillan, 1999).

Murray, Janet H., *Hamlet on the Holodeck: The Future of Narrative in Cyberspace* (New York: The Free Press, 1997).

Nandy, A., *The Intimate Enemy: Loss and Recovery of Self Under Colonialism* (Delhi: Oxford Press, 1983).

Nead, Lynda, *The Female Nude, Art, Obscenity and Sexuality* (London and New York: Routledge, 1992).

Nir, Yeshayahu, 'Photographic Representations and Social Interaction; The Case of The Holy Land' in *History of Photography*, Vol. 19: N. 3, 1995.

Obrist, Hans-Ulrich, 'Soo-Ja Kim: Wrapping Bodies and Souls', *Flash Art*, no. 92, Jan–Feb 1997.

Obrist, Hans-Ulrich, An Interview for the exhibition catalogue: 'Inclusions / Exclusions', Graz, 1996.

Oh Kwang Soo, *A Return to the Archetype: Recent Works of Soo Ja Kim*, essay for exhibition catalogue, Gallery Hyundai, Seoul, 1991.

Papastergiadis, Nikos, *Dialogues in the Diasporas – Essays and Conversations on Cultural Identity* (London: Rivers Oram Press, 1998).

Parker, Rozsika, *Subversive Stitch: Embroidery and Making of the Feminine* (London: The Women's Press Limited, 1984).

Peretz, Don, *Intifada: The Palestinian Uprising* (London: Westview Press, 1990).

Phelan, Peggy, *Mourning Sex. Performing Public Memories* (USA: Routledge, 1997).

Pughe, D.L., Unpublished writing.

Randolph, Jeanne (ed.), *The City Within* (Banff, Alberta: Banff Centre for the Arts, 1992),

Rich, Adrienne, *The Fact of a Doorframe. Poems Selected and New 1950–1982* (New York London: W.W. Norton and Co, 1984).

Roberts, Claire (ed.), *Evolution & Revolution – Chinese Dress 1700s–1990s* (Sydney: Powerhouse Publishing, 1997).

Rose, Barbara, *Magdalena Abakanowicz* (New York: H.N. Abrams, 1994).

Rowley, Sue, 'Warping the Loom: Theoretical Frameworks for Craft Writing', in Noris Ioannou (ed), *Craft in Society: An Anthology of Perspectives* (Australia: South Fremantle Arts Centre Press, 1992).

Silverman, Kaja, 'Fragments of a Fashionable Discourse', in Modleski (ed), *Studies in Entertainment* (Bloomington and Indianapolis: Indiana University Press, 1986).

Stewart, Susan, 'From the Museum of Touch', in Marius Kwint, Christopher Breward, Jeremy Aynsley (eds), *Material Memories: Design and Evocation* (Oxford, England: Berg, 1999).

Sturken, Marita, *Tangled Memories: The Vietnam War, the AIDS Epidemic, and the Politics of Remembering* (Berkeley: University of California, 1997).

Swedenberg, Ted, 'The Palestinian Peasant as National Signifier' in *Anthropological Quarterly*. Vol. 63: No.1. 1990.

Tamari, Selim, 'Soul of the Nation: The Fallah in the Eyes of the Urban Intelligentsia' in Bowman, G. (ed), *Review of Middle East Studies*, London, 1991.

Tarlo, Emma, *Clothing Matters* (Chicago: University of Chicago Press, 1996).

The Hanson Phenomenon, http://www.gwb.com.au/gwb/news/photo /phtalk

Thue, Anniken, Frida Hansen – *en europeer i norsk tekstilkunst omkring* 1900./Frida Hansen – a *European in Norwegian textile around 1900* (Oslo: Universitetsforlaget A/S, 1986).

Tolstrup, Lisbeth, *Grete Balle – Tekstilkunstner og billedskaber /Textile artist and Imagemaker* (Copenhagen: Borgen Publishing, 1996).

Tolstrup, Lisbeth; Ørom, Anette and Graae, Annette (eds), *Tekstilkunst i Danmark 1988–1998/ Textile Art in Denmark 1988–1998* (Copenhagen: Borgen Publishing, 1999).

Truitt, Anne, *Day: The Journey of an Artist* (New York: Patheon, 1982).

Truitt, Anne, *Prospect: The Journey of an Artist* (New York: Putnam, 1996)

Truitt, Anne, *Turn: The Journey of an Artist* (New York: Thames and Hudson, 1979).

Waines, David, 'Failure of the Nationalist Resistance' in Lughod, A.I. (ed), *The Transformation of Palestine; Essays on the Origins and Development of the Arab-Israeli Conflict* (Evanston: Northwestern University Press, 1971).

Warnock, Kitty, *Land Before Honour: Palestinian Women in the Occupied Territories* (London: Macmillan Education Ltd., 1990).

Weir, Shelagh, *Palestinian Costume* (London: British Museum Press, 1994).

Whitford, Margaret, *Luce Irigaray: Philosophy in the Feminine* (London and New York: Routledge, 1991).

Wilson, Elizabeth, *Adorned in Dreams: Fashion and Modernity* (London: Virago, 1987).

Winnicott, D.W., *Playing and Reality* (London: Tavistock, 1971).

Woolf, Virginia, *A Room of One's Own* (London: Penguin, 1928).

Young, G. Elise, 'A Feminist Politics of Healthcare: The case of Palestinian Women Under Israeli Occupation, 1979–1982' in Mayer, T. (ed), *Women and the Israeli Occupation; The Politics of Change* (London and New York: Routledge, 1994).

Yuval-Davis, Nira, 'National Reproduction and The Demographic Race in Israel' in Yuval-Davis & Anthias, F (eds), *Woman-Nation-State* (London: Macmillan, 1989).